# GEORGE HEARST, CALIFORNIA PIONEER

## WESTERNLORE GREAT WEST AND INDIAN SERIES XXXI

1820

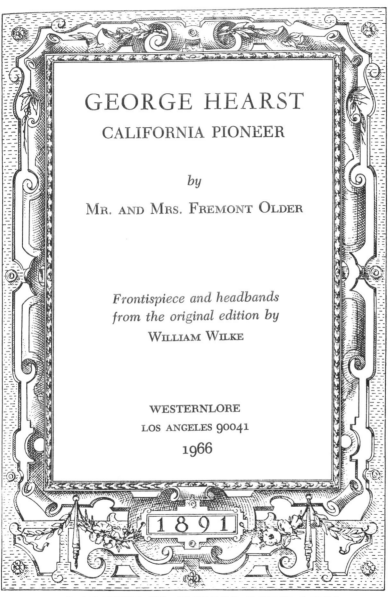

# GEORGE HEARST

## CALIFORNIA PIONEER

*by*

MR. AND MRS. FREMONT OLDER

*Frontispiece and headbands
from the original edition by*
WILLIAM WILKE

WESTERNLORE
LOS ANGELES 90041
1966

1891

# GEORGE HEARST, CALIFORNIA PIONEER

# INTRODUCTION

M̲y husband, Fremont Older and I were on our long desired trip to Europe when we first met a member of the Hearst family. It was late in April 1903, and our ship was the *Kaiser Wilhelm II*. Despite the vessel's size, I was so seasick that for two days I could neither eat nor sleep. Fremont, a better sailor than I, strolled on the deck where he met Mr. William Randolph Hearst who, the day before the ship sailed, had been married to beautiful Miss Millicent Willson. At that time Fremont was editor of the *San Francisco Bulletin*, which often disagreed politically with Hearst's *Examiner*.

Fremont told Mr. Hearst of my seasickness. Mr. Hearst said he had a vacant stateroom that was to have been occupied by Governor James Budd, but at the last moment the Governor had been unable to leave Sacramento. Graciously he said we might have the Governor's stateroom.

I staggered up to the large royal stateroom, and the nausea vanished. The next day I met Mr. and Mrs.

Hearst, and thanked them for making my journey a delight.

We did not meet the Hearsts again until 1918, when Fremont became the editor of *The Call*, which was owned by Mr. Hearst. He invited us to New York, and offered Fremont the editorship of one of his New York papers. We were living on our ranch in sunny Santa Clara County and Fremont couldn't think of leaving our delightful home for noisy New York. He preferred to remain in San Francisco and edit *The Call*.

Early in 1930 Mr. Hearst wired Fremont that he wished him to write the biography of his father—not a eulogy—but to portray Senator George Hearst as he was.

When Mr. Hearst's telegram came, Fremont was writing editorials and in the thick of political battles and he did not see how he could find time to write a biography. I had already had three novels published and I was working on another. Fremont asked me to put aside the novel, and write the life of Senator Hearst. I was from New York, and had never been in the Mother Lode country, and knew nothing about mines, but Fremont said he would drive me to the country where Senator Hearst had made his fortune.

Since my husband's idea of punctuality was to be fifteen minutes ahead of time, we started at 4:30 one morning and reached Placerville at noon. After lunch we went to Pleasant Valley, Diamond Springs and Jackass Gulch. The Mayor of Grass Valley guided us to the LeCompton, Hearst's first important quartz mine. We asked so many questions of those we met that one of the ladies asked, "Are you running for office?"

After three days we were back at our ranch. The next

day we visited the Apperson ranch, near Alviso, which belonged to Senator Hearst's mother-in-law, Mrs. Randolph Apperson. She showed us art objects given by her daughter, Phoebe. Most cherished of all her possessions were "Willie's" baby clothes and his high chair. She told us of how once, when he was there on a visit, he wandered away and the family were in a panic because Willie was lost. All the countryside turned out to look for him. Finally he was found near Alviso. He would always have a desire to see the world.

I worked many months on the 201-page biography. Fremont read each chapter, corrected, and made suggestions, as did Mr. Hearst.

Finally the book was finished. The first volume was bound in white morocco, and weighed five pounds. The pages measured nine by fourteen inches. On August 28, 1933, we arrived at noon at the thirty million dollar castle, *San Simeon*, where there were 150 guests from all over the United States, Hearst had 1000 printed copies of the biography, and each guest was presented with a book.

No book ever made its debut in a setting of such gaiety and luxury as did the Senator Hearst biography. The Castle guests, many of whom were famous, honored the occasion by donning hastily assembled costumes in the Mother Lode styles of '49. Full skirts and sunbonnets brightened the medieval grandeur of fabulous *San Simeon*. Fremont, wearing a sombrero and mining outfit, made the presentation speech. America's most widely read columnist, Arthur Brisbane, also spoke. Then, surprised and delighted by the unexpected costuming of his guests, Mr. Hearst, although wearing a plain brown business suit, contributed to the gaiety by dancing a jig.

At William Randolph Hearst's death in 1951, America's most famed Castle was left to the State of California.

Due to the weight and size of the book, I fear it was little read by the guests who received copies that day. After thirty-two years it has been suggested that the biography of Senator Hearst be copyrighted and published in more readable form.

Since its writing I have been unable to return to fiction. The story of the pioneer who, with only two years of schooling was able to give more than fifty millions to education and philanthropy, and also to serve as United States Senator, is more romantic than any imaginable work of fiction.

—CORA M. OLDER.

# THE FIRST CHAPTER

THE name Hearst is as old as the Saxon race. In Anglo-Saxon it was spelled Hyrst. It meant thicket, or a group of trees. Now the word is frequently used as a termination in local names: as Chiselhurst, Midhurst. The armorial bearings of Hurst of Clough and Howorth consists of a crest, "A hirst of trees," and the motto, "The sun in its splendor."

The American Hearsts were Scotch Presbyterians. Charles II did not like Covenanters. They were sternly moral, and Charles II, with his dancing duchesses, had little use for austere morals. The Covenanters were hunted, imprisoned, tortured, shot and hanged. They regarded persecution as the mysterious working of God's Will. Death was a glorious martyrdom. They would not retaliate. Persecution of them was God's way of testing their souls.

Finally Lauderdale and Claverhouse goaded the Covenanters into open rebellion against Charles. They took up arms. In May 1679, they were defeated by Claverhouse at Dromclog. It was predestined, God's Will. Only a short month later the Covenanters were routed by Charles II's illegitimate son, the Duke of Monmouth, at Bothwell Bridge on the Clyde. The political power of the Kirk was broken.

Persecution went on. For these defeated Presbyterians there were only ruin, desolation and death in Scotland. They turned their despairing eyes across the Atlantic to the colonies. There was hope, freedom to worship God as they pleased. At last they understood the mysterious working of Divine Will. The Hearsts sailed for the American colonies.

Most of the Covenanters who fled across the ocean after the disastrous battle of Bothwell Bridge settled first in New York and Pennsylvania. Many of them gradually moved from these colonies into the western parts of Virginia and the Carolinas. Some established themselves at Port Royal, South Carolina. Spaniards from Saint Augustine in 1686 completely destroyed Port Royal. The survivors of this disaster went north and west to the safer communities.

The founder of the Hearst, or Hurst, family in America was John Hurst of the Isle of Wight County, Virginia. He arrived in the American colonies in 1680. There is a tradition that he acquired ten acres of land and nine negro slaves. John Hurst was a pioneer in a region that rewarded only the masterful, those undaunted by danger and hardships. His will of 1727 named the following children: James, John, William, Philip, Walter, Alicia and Mary. The sons of John Hurst moved to Edgecombe and Bertie Counties, North Carolina. In Bertie County the old spelling of Hurst for the first time was changed to Hearst. John Hearst III, in the colonies, was the great-grandfather of George Hearst of Biglow, Franklin County, Missouri, and of San Francisco.

John Hearst married a North Carolinian. His first wife, Elizabeth Knox, was the mother of all his children. His second wife was Mary, widow of a James O'Brien. In 1776, just as the Declaration of Independence was declared, John Hearst moved with his family to South Carolina and took out his first land patent in what later became Abbeville County, on the western border of the state, adjoining Georgia. He was a resident of the Long Cane section of Abbeville County when he made his will in 1780. It was probated in 1782, giving the name sof his eleven children: Robert, John, Joseph, Thomas, George, William, Mary, Christian, Elizabeth, Margaret and Ann. The second son, John, was a major in the Continental Army. This son had ten children. The third son, Joseph, had nine. The Hearsts were a clannish family. Three of John Hearst's daughters married three brothers of the Pressly family, all of them Presbyterian clergymen. One hundred years in the new world had only strengthened the devotion of the Hearst family to Kirk and Covenant. George Hearst, fifth son of John Hearst III, had four children who lived to maturity. His eldest son was William G. Hearst, father of George Hearst of San Francisco.

From the time the Hearsts uprooted themselves from Scotland for the sake of their faith, they were men of vision, strong courageous, always looking beyond, always seeking new frontiers. The Hearsts prospered and multiplied. They acquired land. With musket and grit they defended their holdings. A record in the early nineteenth century tells of land litigation in Texas. The Hearsts successfully resisted the spoilers. They were

Scotch Covenanters to the bone, thrifty and hard working. They toiled early and late, and accumulated money that their children might enjoy the advantages developing with the growth of America. The Hearsts would not have been Scotch Covenanters had they lacked a passionate desire for learning. One Hearst left one thousand dollars—a great sum in his day—in order that a promising nephew might complete his education.

Earnest as were the Hearsts in their desire to increase the family fortunes, they were not so tenacious of what they acquired that they hesitated to hazard it when attractive opportunities offered. Theirs was the spirit of America—the desire to look beyond, to widen their acres and their horizon. They were in a new land where new work was before them. The new work was done by settlers who refused to "settle down." These men and women had so much faith in the land of their choice that when they brought it to harvest in one region they moved on to prepare another wilderness for the plow. The Hearsts were westering pioneers.

In 1803 America became a new America. Thomas Jefferson paid Napoleon fifteen million dollars for Louisiana. Immediately there was another flight westward. A fresh tide of immigration flowed across the Mississippi into Missouri, then called upper Louisiana, fabled for two centuries as the land of gold and silver.

In the new territory of upper Louisiana there was no ban on slaveholding; and so Kentucky, Tennessee, Georgia, Virginia and the Carolinas contributed their best to this new western empire. Some of these pioneers sought success they had not known in their home states, but many of the families brought traditions of gentility, slaves, symbols of comfortable or luxurious living. In this new Louisiana each hoped to give his children greater security for the future than the home states offered.

William Hearst of Abbeville County, South Carolina, heard of upper Louisiana, where "milk and honey flowed" and where there were gold and silver. He read the letters of the first adventurers. He listened to the tales brought back by scouts, drovers and river-men. He was greatly interested, but his Scotch caution caused him to wait five years before he disturbed the peace of his household gods and set out for upper Louisiana, later called Missouri.

In 1808 William Hearst trekked across Kentucky, following the steps of Daniel Boone, who had gone on ahead in 1803. Hearst visited St. Louis, then a trading post in northern Louisiana, took the ferry across the Mississippi River, crowded with a continuous line of wagons moving from the east into the newly opened western country. He went into St. Louis County, a portion of which later was to be named Franklin County, to honor the great Benjamin Franklin.

William Hearst was an excellent judge of land. He knew just what he wanted. He journeyed into that part of the country where Daniel Boone and the early French trappers had tarried. This was where the Ozark Plateau slopes to the Mississippi. Everywhere were Indians. In this country were several hundred Indian tepees, but many of the French settlers had intermarried with the natives, and so they inspired no fear.

William Hearst liked to breathe a little above the sea level. In hills he found exaltation. He was lured by far vistas. He was most attracted by the Ridge in Franklin

County, varying from five hundred to one thousand feet in altitude and running from the northeast to the southwest. All the streams on one side flowed to the Missouri, and on the other to the Meramec. He chose the Meramec side. He saw that on the east and southeast stretched a principality to the Gulf of Mexico. Directly south was the beautiful valley to be named the Arkansas Valley. North and northeast the plateau dropped to the Missouri and the majestic Mississippi. North and west were endless prairies. It all pleased his eye. He computed the sugar and syrup to be obtained from large maple trees. He wandered through forests of oak, ash, walnut, hickory, elm. He sat under the sprawling dappled gray sycamores by the stream. He knew that corn would grow rank in the valleys and on the terraced land. He sensed that there also would thrive wheat, oats and rye. He knew that the nutritious wild grass on the thinnest clay hill land would afford excellent pasturage. He guessed that fruits would come to perfection wherever he planted. These undulating uplands delighted the observant planter, and bade him remain.

Perhaps William Hearst overlooked that much ground had been eroded to extreme ruggedness. He was not conscious that here would be found iron, copper and lead. He was not a mining man. He was a man of the soil. Here was land rich and cheap, and here he would make his home. He took up land along the pleasant Meramec River.

Hearst was mostly interested in the cultivation of wheat and corn. In 1808 there was a market for these cereals in St. Louis, which boasted of a population of almost five thousand. At first, there was no means of transporting cereals to consumers forty miles away, and so Hearst raised food solely for his domestic needs. Later he sold to his less industrious neighbors. His greatest profit came from horses and cattle driven into St. Louis. He sold these to trappers and traders. In the St. Louis market he purchased some slaves. Each year he bought more land. Life smiled for the young pioneer.

The Hearsts have never married young, but shortly after William Hearst took up his land on the Meramec River, he was attracted by the daughter of a neighbor, Elizabeth Collins, daughter of Jacob Collins. Elizabeth was born in Georgia. Her parents had moved to Biglow in 1805, three years before the arrival of young Hearst. Elizabeth Collins brought to any occasion grace, charm, liveliness, and a delightful whimsical humor. When there was a corn-husking she was the one who made it like a festival. A quilting bee at the Collins' house was never an ordinary quilting bee. When there was a Fourth of July picnic, and a speaker came from St. Louis to deliver the oration and bid for the rural vote, the Collins family entertained him. Traveling preachers liked to stop at the Collins' house. Elizabeth read the weekly St. Louis paper and a ladies' magazine. She could talk about the Bible. She could talk about life.

When William Hearst was working in the field or riding through the forest he often thought of Elizabeth Collins, with her clear healthy skin, her regular features, her deep blue eyes, her sunny hair, her impressive height, her rich, gently modulated voice and her serene well-poised manner. Sometimes she went riding with him. She rode with grace, as did Hearst himself. They both loved horses, and horses were their servants. Elizabeth's clothes were different from those of other women of the frontier. She had brought with her from Georgia Leghorn bonnets and cashmere shawls and bits of lace that often fluttered at her throat.

As soon as William Hearst felt able to marry he asked Elizabeth to be his wife. It was the day of his greatest fortune. In 1817 Mr. and Mrs. William G. Hearst rode up to St. Louis on their wedding journey, and to see the first steamer arrive on the Mississippi River. When they returned, all the neighbors for miles around came to help them roll the logs and "raise" the new Hearst log cabin.

With Elizabeth Collins as his wife, to Hearst that log cabin never seemed quite like other log cabins. He often wondered how she ever did all the things that she accomplished. She was calm, good humored, smiling, friendly. Her excellent advice spurred him forward. Elizabeth Collins Hearst didn't waste time fearing the crops would go wrong, or that her husband couldn't sell the cattle. If things did go wrong, they would be all right the next time. She always saw the humorous side and she never worried if the neighbors did foolish things or worked on Sunday. She was not shocked by the pranks of the neighborhood children. She thought that people were much better than the critical ones said. She knew how to manage her work. She never repeated her steps, nor became confused when visitors came unexpectedly and there wasn't as much in the larder as she would have liked. She had a genius for finding vegetables growing in the garden that others couldn't see, and berries underneath the vines that others couldn't find, and hens' eggs tucked away that escaped other eyes. She expected things to go right, and they did.

William Hearst often said his wife had a twenty-six hour day instead of twenty-four. She cooked, kept the house neat, cured ham and bacon, raised chickens, ducks and geese, made goose-feather pillows and goose-feather beds for the St. Louis market, pieced quilts exquisitely, wove cloth out of cotton and wool, made bedding, towels, her own clothing and her husband's. She cured the hides of animals shot by him, made tallow candles, attended to the vegetable garden, gathered wild berries, and had a medicine chest with herbal remedies for every disease known in the neighborhood. She sat up with the sick horses. Once she nursed a chicken, a cat, a dog and a horse the same day. She never distinguished between helping white people and black, or dumb animals, or Indians who wandered in each summer to visit them. They all liked her. Perhaps they liked her because she liked them. She was a lady, but she was not conscious of it; nor was she aware that she was a great democrat and a great human being.

Elizabeth Collins Hearst did so much and with such ease and grace during the first three years of their married life that William Hearst wondered if his wife could possibly find time for one more occupation. Could she find time to be a mother?

In 1820 motherhood approached. Elizabeth Collins Hearst wove enough little garments to fill an Indian basket. She was happy when her handsome, rugged, blue-eyed first born, her son George, came. Often she did her work carrying him on her left hip while she worked with her right arm. This man-child of Elizabeth Hearst's was never a burden to her. From the beginning he seemed like her very self. He, too, was smiling and friendly and strong. He looked out on the world with pleasant happy blue eyes. Whenever unhappiness and disappointment came he met them with calm courage. He was Elizabeth Collins Hearst's own son. Years later, after George Hearst had made fifteen millions in fifteen years, and had gone to the United States Senate, and had become a mining seer pointing the way to men delving into the mysteries of the bowels of the earth, he reviewed his long life and said: "My father was a very industrious man, but I believe I owe most of my success to my mother."

Without Elizabeth Collins Hearst probably there never would have been the genius-geologist, George Hearst.

# THE SECOND CHAPTER

W HEN George Hearst was born in 1820, Napoleon, the caged lion, was roaring from St. Helena at fat King George IV of England. In 1820 Charles Dickens was a child labeling blacking pots in London. In 1820 Byron was writing poetry in Ravenna. In 1820 eleven-year-old Abe Lincoln was sleeping on a bed of boughs in the loft of a one room cabin belonging to his father in the wilderness of Indiana. In 1820 Monroe had just been re-elected President. He had brought about the Missouri Compromise, the first peaceful adjustment of slavery; but ships kept on sailing to Africa with sugar and calico and returning with "niggers." However, slavery was not of great importance to the Hearst family.

When George Hearst was three years old he was given a little sister, Martha, nicknamed "Patsy." He wished she was a boy, but he loved to carry the baby in his strong arms. Then came a brother, Philip, a cripple from birth, but with a beautiful face like that of their mother. From the beginning George was compelled to be independent and helpful. He was glad not to be a burden to his mother. She called him "mother's boy." He was proud when she said he would always be her "stay."

George Hearst was a child of the wilderness. There were no schools in Franklin County. School districts were not formed until 1845. The boy never went to church, because no church was built until 1836, and that was Roman Catholic. So he was taught largely by life. He helped his father, who worked harder than even black people. As William Hearst's family increased, the hours of his toil lengthened. George was with him when he cultivated the fields, when he ran his country store. George went with him when he attended political meetings. The lad enjoyed the cheers and music, and he even kept awake during the speeches. William Hearst took a great interest in public affairs. He was first lieutenant of the militia. George liked to see his father wear his lieutenant's uniform, and to go with him when there was a parade.

George also shared his mother's work. He looked after her ducks and chickens. He gathered the eggs, and set the hens. He helped his mother pull the feathers from the geese for feather beds and pillows. Sometimes she had more feathers than they could use, and he was delighted when she sold nice, soft goose-feather pillows and beds. Early he began cutting kindling wood for her, and he was glad when he learned to chop large chunks for the fireplace.

Elizabeth Collins Hearst told her boy that she was sorry he had to do so much work. She wished he could go to school and learn the three R's. She hoped for a public school in Franklin County. He helped her clean and card the wool, of which she made clothing for a family of five. It was an endless task to beat out cotton and flax seed, but he liked it. He enjoyed helping her spin and weave. He was glad to hold her thread balls. George Hearst never felt that his mother's cloth was like that of any other woman's weaving. It was his own triumph when people said she was the best spinner and weaver in the neighborhood. Little George Hearst thought he had the smartest mother in the world. In the first eight years of his life he decided that he must be a very smart man himself to keep up with his handsome mother, and make her proud of him, as he was of her. She told him that she did not know what she should do without him. That was the highest praise he knew. Once when he disobeyed her, she came toward him with a stick. She did not strike him, but he was always sad when he thought of that disobedience.

George Hearst did not go to school, but after he finished work he hunted, fished, swam and paddled in the shallow places in the river. His mother frowned on his hunting or fishing on Sundays. She told him it was not "very nice," but she seldom scolded or was cross. She liked to see the children play. She was sorry they did not have more time for fun. She regretted that George had to do a man's work, though she was grateful to him for helping his father. She encouraged him in games. Often when he rode his father's horses he imagined he was an Indian chief. He frequently saw Indians, especially when he went to help his father drive the hogs to market. Often Indians came to the house for food.

One fall when George Hearst was eight or nine his

mother was very happy. A teacher with a book and ferule opened a school in the spare room of a neighbor's house. It was great news for Elizabeth Hearst. From miles distant the children came. George Hearst was accustomed to hard work. Learning lessons at the new academy seemed like play. George was sorry he could not attend school every day, but he learned rapidly. He found arithmetic especially interesting. Those three months of schooling unlocked the mysteries of newspapers and books, and his world was never the same again.

In the following year George Hearst, for the first time, went to St. Louis to visit his aunt. It was a memorable event for the boy to see the boats on the Mississippi and to cross on the ferry. He had never seen so many people before, nor so richly dressed. He wished his mother were with him, wearing her prettiest dress and bonnet, so everyone could see how handsome she was. It was the first time he had ever been without work to do. He missed the log cabin home on the Meramec, his sister and his crippled brother. He wondered about the chickens, ducks and geese. He wondered if the wolves would kill any of the sheep. Who would pen the sheep in the fold? What would become of his pet lamb?

When George visited his aunt she was pleased that he knew something about reading, writing and arithmetic. That first night when she tucked him in his bed, she asked him to say his prayers. George couldn't say his prayers. Aunt was horrified. She felt that she had a lost soul in the house. The boy was taught his prayers; he was taken to church. Learning to read, and learning to pray, were two of the great events of George Hearst's childhood. They disclosed to him beautiful, significant, unrevealed worlds. But he was glad to return to the log cabin. He was more free. So long as he lived he chafed under restraint.

As George Hearst grew older it was more difficult for him to attend school, because each day brought some new tasks. He had to milk cows, watch the sheep, look after the hogs, help prepare them for market. He became a father's boy, as well as a mother's boy, and went everywhere with William Hearst. In fact, he learned all his father's occupations. He worked with his father and the slaves in the corn.

There was a demand for William Hearst's hogs from the French overseers and lead miners not fifteen miles away. It was difficult to drive hogs fifteen miles over rough roads, but going to the mines was always a treat to George. The diggings and the smelters fascinated the boy. George Hearst came to know the French miners very well. They liked him, and the Frenchmen, with their keen human sense, were especially attracted to the manly, observant, handsome boy. They sensed a high intelligence in him, and tried to teach him their language. Bashfully he struggled to please them. When he succeeded the miners rewarded him with little gifts. Once they gave him a five franc piece. He always kept it.

The miners took George down into the lead mines. He had no fear of the earth. Even as a boy he went down into the miners' caves forty feet deep. This pleased the Frenchmen. They took him to their homes, and showed him undreamed-of grandeurs. George had known only log houses, with beds and chairs of the simplest pioneer make. He was dazzled by the beauty and grace of the miners' French furniture. Tenderly he touched satin-wood, rosewood. He thought it wonderful to be rich and and have furniture like the Frenchmen. What a beautiful country France must be!

In 1853 a new lead mine was discovered at St. Clair, only a mile from the Hearst home. It was named the Virginia, and it proved to be an excellent mine. Today it is the "Old Virginia." The Virginia was the lode star for the neighborhood youngsters, something for them to dream about. George Hearst later said: "The miners would not wash anything out, but let us little fellows pick into the big banks of dirt. We used to dig down and get free bits of lead. Sometimes we made from four to six bits a day."

When George Hearst dug down into the Virginia Mine for the lead fragments he did not realize that his real career, and his real education, had begun.

# THE THIRD CHAPTER

V ERY early in life George Hearst was fascinated about exploring the earth. The Indians named him "Boy-That-Earth-Talks-To." He was never more happy than when he visited the great Fischer's Cave, near Staunton, in the Meramec River bluff. He wondered constantly about what was in the earth. Here was a chance for him to see natural caves abounding in curious formations. He went with his father and some neighbors through a crooked gallery a mile long, varying in height from five to fifteen feet. It was a hundred feet in diameter, set with masses of beautiful, hanging, tapering icicle-like stalactites suspended from the vaulted ceiling. Century after century they had dripped slowly in the silence of the cavern and had formed stately stalagmites.

Another great experience was his going to see Jacob's Well, near Detmold. He could not forget the thrill and wonder of seeing the well opening downward through eighty feet of stone. There a large lake opened out, roofed with stone, at the height of twenty-five feet. The mines, the cave, the well, made him think much about what was concealed in the earth, made him long to know more.

The boy questioned his father and mother. Elizabeth Hearst taught him all she knew. She wished she knew more. Each year she hoped that he would be able to go to school again. George tried to puzzle out books, and he longed to learn as much as the teacher knew. But each year his father had more work to do, each year he bought new slaves, his acreage increased. Finally William Hearst had one hundred and fifty acres cleared and under cultivation, but he never had enough men to do his work. It seemed to him the time would never come when he wouldn't need George. In fact, he would have liked a large family of boys to carry out his plans and projects. If little, wistful, beautiful Philip could work. but he couldn't. George tried to work for himself and Philip too.

George Hearst passed fourteen before he was again able to go to school. He had never been so happy as when his father told him that he could study for a whole year. The school lasted fifteen months, and George attended with fair regularity. To the days he spent in those rude cabin classrooms he eagerly added laborious nights of study. So feverish was his desire to learn that he could hardly tear himself away from the schoolroom.

Several years later George Hearst's teacher, Mr. Berry, recalled to him how he used to remain after school and worry over his lessons. Often Berry came back and found the boy still in the schoolroom intensely struggling to master new tasks. The teacher said it was very hard to send the pupil away. Berry used to say that George Hearst was the first pupil in all his experience who did not try to shirk a lesson if he thought he could not learn it. He also said that he never knew any other pupil who was willing to work after time. The teacher added that another characteristic of George Hearst was that after he began learning arithmetic he never did a sum according to rule. He always figured it out in his own way, or not at all.

George Hearst later said that this was his tendency throughout life. At school he never accomplished anything that he did not work for. After he finished his arithmetic, Berry asked George to take it home with him to see if he could work out the sums at the end of the book. Berry found that the boy could do all of them, because he knew the principle. Few pupils, the teacher said, if any, were able to do this.

After George Hearst was fifteen there came to him five years of barren longing for an education, but he was unable to go to school until he was twenty. Then he attended but three or four months. Contact with life did the rest. His entire school attendance covered two years. Abraham Lincoln went to school only one year.

At times George Hearst felt cheated. There were so many books he longed to read. There was so much that he wished to do besides raise hogs and cattle and drive them to the market. He grew sick of sweating with the Negroes in the wheat and corn fields. He remained alone on his father's lower farm, and worked it from the time he was sixteen. His great strength, energy and capacity were bursting to escape this limited life. Somewhere in the world he was certain there was a chance for him to achieve. He read the newspapers; he read about rough President Jackson and the Indian war in Randolph County, the doings of Congress, the threatened revolt in Texas, the border struggles in Mexico. Sometimes he told his mother of his ambitions. More rarely he mentioned them to his father.

"George," his father answered, "I'll buy another farm. I'll open a store. Philip is an invalid. When I'm gone, you can have it all."

William Hearst did buy another farm. He bought until he owned eight hundred acres. He opened a country store. Farming, cattle raising, storekeeping filled the boy's days, but did not really satisfy his dreams. There must be something for him far from Biglow on the Meramec, something that differed as greatly as the polished inlaid furniture of the French mine owners differed from the crude pioneer tables and chairs of Franklin County.

George Hearst climbed the highest tree on his father's farm, where the Ozark Plateau slopes to the Mississippi River. Here was a space of open splendor. Lifted a thousand feet above sea level, he looked east and southeast to the Gulf of Mexico; south to the Arkansas Valley; north and northeast to the Missouri and the Mississippi, and to the Shawnee Hills beyond—then, west to the wide prairies. He wondered what lay over there beyond the Rockies and the Sierra Nevada in California, slumbering on the Pacific under the flag of Mexico. Would George Hearst ever go there?

## THE FOURTH CHAPTER

In 1846, just as the Mexican flag fell over California, and the Stars and Stripes were raised at Monterey, William Hearst died, ten thousand dollars in debt. He had been too kind to his neighbors, given too lavishly when they were in need or managed less well than he. In the friendly pioneer fashion of South Carolina and frontier Missouri he had pledged the security of his name for considerable sums.

Elizabeth Hearst was a widow, and penniless. Patsy was i her teens. Philip was a helpless cripple.

In that grim desolate hour the gently bred Elizabeth Collins Hearst, who so liberally had given her youth and strength to her husband, now had no strength save in her twenty-six year old son, George. The young man recalled to his mother that she had taught him as a boy to pen the sheep in the fold to protect them from the wolves. Now he would keep the wolves of hunger and poverty away from his mother, sister and helpless brother. Elizabeth, Patsy and Philip clung to George in their grief.

Their family love was deepened and intensified by death. No other life was possible to George but the life of his brother, sister and mother.

George Hearst had mastered his arithmetic by stubbornly refusing to shirk the difficult. Now life presented him its knottiest problem. He would solve this, too. His brother, sister and mother gave him all their faith. They knew.

After Elizabeth Collins Hearst became a widow her neighbors, the Randolph Appersons, a family of considerable culture, sustained her with sympathy and friendship. The Appersons had been friends of the Hearsts ever since they arrived from Virginia. Their little daughter, Phoebe Elizabeth, had been named for George's own mother, Elizabeth Collins Hearst.

This child was like an exquisite bit of porcelain. George Hearst and she were great friends. He liked her for her lovely, delicate features, her serious gray-blue eyes, her exquisiteness. The family called her "Puss." Often George Hearst carried the child on his horse to visit his mother, taking her into the house on his shoulder. Elizabeth Collins Hearst loved her. Phoebe was the pet of the Hearst family. George Hearst felt toward her much as he did for the lovely inlaid furniture in the house of the French mining superintendent. Phoebe Apperson seemed to belong with marqueterie. The child was like a lovely flower to the eyes of the struggling farmer and storekeeper.

George Hearst managed the three heavily encumbered farms. He directed the work of four slaves and several hired men. He sold cattle. His stock commanded the best prices, for he was instinctively keen in judging and breeding horses. During the harvests his reaping hook hastened the reaping hooks of the slaves and hired men. Always he felt the burden of debt, and the ache of that debt on the shoulders of his mother. To eke out their family income, for a time George ran a little country store on the "Old Springfield Road." Storekeeping, farming and cattle dealing in the eighteen hundred and forties in Franklin County, Missouri, gave little profit. George began devising ways out of his inherited financial difficulty. In those days ten thousand dollars was a colossal sum.

Elizabeth Hearst tried to help the family fortunes by selling poultry and by weaving, but she accomplished little. Her heart sank with that of her son. She recalled that she often heard her husband say if he saved two hundred dollars a year he was doing well.

Hearst, as the Indians said, was The-Boy-That-Earth-Talked-To. Instinctively his ideas turned to mining. To him the earth was no mystery. It was his friend. He was fascinated by tracing conformations. He had a keen perception of the strata of the earth. From boyhood Hearst felt that the only business romance in Franklin County was lead mining and lead miners. Although he knew nothing about geology, he turned to lead mining. Daily the lead miners performed the alchemy of making money easily. Hearst was to become the greatest practical mining geologist of his time. Even in his questioning youth he felt that when he asked of the earth its mysteries, the earth would answer.

Hearst sought advice of a neighbor, Doctor Silas Reed, a physician from St. Louis who had settled in Franklin County because he owned a lead mine. Doctor Reed was reputed to be deeply versed in geology and mineralogy. He lent George Hearst books on geology and mineralogy. The young man devoured them eagerly, passionately. He did not put them down until late into the night. He was reading for a more beautiful life, freedom from debt, love of his brother, sister and mother. It was his new way of penning the sheep in the fold to protect those he loved from new wolves.

From Doctor Reed's books on geology and mineralogy, George Hearst turned to the lead mines and verified in nature all he had read. Lead mining was the first industry in Missouri. By nearly a half century it preceded the establishment in 1764 of the fur trading post at St. Louis by Chouteau and Laclede. Lead mines had been worked by the French ever since the first lead mine, Mine La Motte, was discovered in 1715 by Antoine Laumet de la Mothe Cadillac, the Governor of Louisiana and the founder of Detroit. Cadillac and Renault came to New Orleans about 1719, bringing two hundred miners, the necessary tools and implements, and a number of slaves picked up in Santo Domingo on the way. They were following the trail of Hernando de Soto, who came in 1541, the first white man to visit Missouri.

Like de Soto, Cadillac and Renault expected to find mines of gold and silver of fabulous richness on the shores of the Mississippi. They began their explorations in what was then called Louisiana, but which is now St. Genevieve County, Missouri. Here they found neither gold nor silver, but almost everywhere lead in abundance. Lead was a necessity among the early settlers of the West. Rifles supplied the food they lived on and defended them against enemies. Lead found a ready market.

In 1741 twenty-five hundred bars or "pigs" of lead were mined in Franklin County, Missouri. Sometimes miners made thirty dollars a day for weeks before a deposit failed. Often in the early Missouri days lead was used as currency. In 1826 Missouri produced almost enough lead to supply all the countries of the world. During thirteen years the Mine La Motte was busily worked. In 1838 the mine was leased to miners in forty acre tracts, from which several million pounds of lead were obtained.

George Hearst frequently visited the Virginia Mine, only a mile away from his house. There he observed that the Frenchmen mined shallow diggings. As Hearst studied them he was more and more persuaded that French mining was not very scientific. As soon as the miners got out a few hundred pounds of ore, they sold it to the smelter and spent the money lavishly.

In those days miners were not even called miners. They were known as "diggers." They dug pits, holes in the earth from ten to forty feet deep. The ore was found in detached masses, from an ounce to several hundred pounds weight.

Small smelting furnaces were erected in suitable situations. In 1789, just as George Washington became President, Moses Austin of Virginia sunk in Franklin County the first regular shaft from which large quantities of lead were taken. His first smelting was crude but effective. A square excavation in the ground was made to the depth of three feet, walled up with straight even logs cut from green trees and joined at the corners after the fashion of a log house. It was covered with similar green timbers. The lead ore was placed within the structure, on a layer of dry wood. When everything was ready the wood was set afire and burned to ashes. The ore was melted and fused into a lump of pure lead.

Hearst concluded that there was a great deal of money being made in lead mining in Missouri. There would be much more if the mines were worked scientifically and economically. He leased lead claims, developed them according to improved methods. He had success with both lead and copper. From 1846 to 1849 he made more money than he had ever dreamed could be earned by him in Franklin County. Philip, his invalid brother, was dead. George paid his father's indebtedness of ten thousand dollars. He was earning enough to keep his mother and sister in comfort.

Those three years gave George Hearst a new profession. He had so many contacts that he was better educated than he would have been had he been taught by a college of mines. In reality, he had laid the foundation of his fortune. He was ready for greater fields.

Just as Hearst finished paying his father's debts, in January 1848, James W. Marshall, in California, saw the blinding flash of gold on the south fork of the American River. That flash changed George Hearst's life, and it made world history.

# THE FIFTH CHAPTER

PRESIDENT Polk in his message to Congress, December 5, 1848, announced that California was rich in gold. The President's message started the great trek across the country. The world went California-mad. What did it matter to youth that deserts and death lay between them and their El Dorado? What did it matter that there was the Sierra to climb, where two years before the Donner party had been frozen and starved into cannibalism? Beyond lay California, with its treasure of gold. The thundering stampede was on.

When the age-old siren, gold, called from sleeping California, Missouri was the first to listen and to answer. From the beginning Missourians were mining men. Once more the dreams of de Soto, Renault and Cadillac were dreamed. Each Missourian felt that he would be a millionaire.

During the entire year of 1849 the youth of Missouri poured into California. Several thousand went from Franklin County and the neighboring counties, Washington and St. Louis. Their echoes came back from the long covered wagon trail to California in the song:

> My name it is Joe Bowers,
> I have a brother Ike:
> I came from old Missouri—
> Came all the way from Pike.

Young George Hearst paused in his work in the lead mines. He longed to go to California, but at first he said little. There were his mother, and his young sister, Patsy. Ever since his father's death, George's hand had held the door against poverty. He heard that in California men were making forty or fifty dollars a day. Suddenly lead mining seemed to him dull, dreary. California was the opportunity for which he had waited.

"Mother," he said suddenly, "I have made up my mind—I am going to California."

Elizabeth Hearst felt as all mothers feel about ventures separating them from an only son. Once more George was the boy who penned in the sheep from the wolves. Who would protect her now? Who would protect him? The wolves he must face were wolves he had never known. What did gold matter? She urged her stalwart, strong, handsome son against the hazard. Perhaps President Polk was deceived; perhaps the stories of California gold deposits were exaggerated; California was more than two thousand miles away. Only a mile distant, there was a lead mine, the Virginia. If George remained at home, maybe he would find another mine. Better lead mines, known and understood so well by him, than those fabled gold mines across the continent. Prairies, deserts, snowy mountains, Indians, California—it all seemed only a trap for her boy.

George Hearst was strong, quiet, determined. He felt in himself the power to grapple with great problems and to meet and control great situations. He believed that a California comes only once in history. There was a lilt in the very word California.

In spite of his enthusiasm, George Hearst's tenderness caused him to conciliate his doubting mother. To please her, he consulted a neighbor named Mannie, an iron worker of some importance in the community. Mannie wished George Hearst to marry his daughter, and he advised him to remain in Missouri.

"There is nothing new in California," said Mannie. "Seventy-five years ago the Jesuits discovered gold there."

Mannie showed Hearst a book that seemed to prove his statement. Perhaps he had a copy of the English version (1759) of a work on California, written by the Jesuit, Miguel Vanegas. That book deals with lower California, but it contains notes to the effect that along the coast of upper California, gold and silver are to be found, as well as in the interior. No gold was found in upper California by the Jesuits; the first Jesuits arrived from Oregon in 1848, and they remained in San Francisco. This fact was unknown to Mannie. Nor did he know that the legend of California was gold; mountains of gold containing caves of gold where Queen Califa and her Amazons once lived. From the beginning the Spanish kings believed that in California were great riches of pearls and gold. This belief inspired the earliest expeditions to the Pacific Coast.

Indians of old had brought from the coast ranges to the Missions small golden ornaments. Even before Marshall's discovery at Coloma, small quantities of gold were taken out of the Sierra Nevada foothills. In 1827, Jedediah Smith, trapper, pathfinder, first American to cross the Sierra, discovered gold, probably in Mono County. In 1843 Captain John A. Sutter and General John Bidwell were shown by a French-Canadian trapper, Baptiste Ruelle, some small particles of gold said to have been found in the American River. Neither Sutter nor Bidwell believed Ruelle. In the following year, Pablo Gutierrez found gold in the Sierra Nevada, and told Bidwell about it. The General made some investigation, but he was half-hearted and skeptical.

Of the one really notable discovery of gold before Marshall it was unlikely that Mannie had heard. Francisco Lopez, a Spanish-Californian had a ranch on Piru Creek, a branch of the Santa Clara River, which enters the ocean a few miles southeast of the City of Buena Ventura. Lopez' discovery was accidental. He had been rounding up cattle on the rancho of Doctor Antonio del Valle, when he stopped for a rest at the San Francisquito Arroyo. With his knife he dug up some wild onions, and on the roots he discovered yellow specks which he knew were gold. This occurred March 9, 1842, at a spot twenty miles northwest of the Mission San Fernando. Lopez formed a partnership with Charles Barec, a Frenchman. They sold their dust in Los Angeles in goose and vulture quills, making six or eight thousand dollars in their venture.

During 1842 and 1843 about two thousand ounces of gold were taken from the creek near San Fernando. Some of these nuggets were sent by Abel Stearns to the mint at Philadelphia, and the rest found their way also to the United States. In 1844 Manuel Castanares reported this discovery to the Mexican government, but the report attracted only passing attention. The small, early gold discoveries in California were quite forgotten in the wild romances of 1849 concerning the richness of the California gold deposits.

In spite of her protests Elizabeth Hearst saw her son surrender to the spell of these tales brought back to Missouri from California. Men lived to be two hundred in California. There was more gold in California than in the ancient cities of Mexico and Peru, where cities were roofed with gold, and temples were hung with golden suns, and heathen gods were entwined with serpents of beaten gold!

George Hearst realized that there were no golden roofs, no golden temples, nor golden mountains in California, nor caves of gold where Queen Califa and her Amazons once lived. But he knew the earth. He had dug into its bowels. He had followed the baffling ways of ledges. The earth talked to him. He made up his mind to ride away in the spring of 1850 to California. He was certain that beyond the plains and deserts and mountains were fortunes for men who were not afraid.

# THE SIXTH CHAPTER

GEORGE HEARST had never been more than forty miles from home when he decided to go to California. His closest friend was his cousin, Joseph Clark. Joseph and his brother, Jacob, decided to go with Hearst. The Clarks were also connections of the Appersons. Eight other men and six women from the vicinity of the Hearst farm made up the party. Hearst outfitted himself and three others, one of them being a young neighbor named Phillips. In order to equip himself for the journey Hearst went to the big city, St. Louis, forty miles distant. At that time it had a population of about seventy thousand.

From Hearst's farming and mining ventures considerable sums of money were due him. He collected what he could, and took notes for the remainder. He gave a lawyer his power-of-attorney. He turned over to his mother and sister sufficient money to provide for them during his absence. Joseph and Jacob Clark, and eight men and six women, went on ahead in covered wagons.

Hearst and Phillips promised, by fast riding, to overtake the Clark wagons on the Big Blue River.

On the day before Hearst set out, he rode to the Randolph Apperson's farm to say goodbye to them, and to little Phoebe Elizabeth Apperson. He asked Mrs. Apperson to visit his mother and sister after he was gone. He gave Phoebe Elizabeth Apperson, only seven years, old, one last ride on his horse. The little girl, with the grave gray-blue eyes, was silent as they rode. She blinked away tears because her big friend was going to far California, perhaps to be killed by Indians.

"Puss, don't cry like a papoose," he said. "I'll send you a nice present from California. But he knew that he might never come back.

On the morning of the twelfth day of May, 1850, the realization that he might never see them again was still strong with him. For the last time he sat down for breakfast in the log house. Even the friendly hounds sensed that this morning was different; their mistress stopped in her morning tasks to wipe her eyes. Elizabeth Hearst was re-living in imagination the story of the ghastly cannibalism of the Donner party in the Sierra in 1846. What would happen to George after he left Missouri? Elizabeth Hearst and Patsy knew it was the last meal they would prepare for George for years, perhaps forever. They wished him to remember it. They gave him fried chicken, hominy, corn bread, bacon and fragrant coffee. The women stood over him and urged him to eat more and more. When the time for parting came, Elizabeth Hearst could not let her boy go alone. She and Patsy decided to ride with George and Phillips a little way. This change of plans was like a reprieve before execution. It made the setting out far easier. The

Negro slaves with their wives and children, came to take leave of their master. As the Negroes bade him goodbye they told him they knew when Marse George came back he "suah" would be the richest man in Missouri.

On the morning of May 12, 1850, George Hearst rode away from the house where he was born. Beside him rode his mother and sister. How cozy and comfortable the old home place looked. How beautiful the Meramec was. He had learned to swim there. He passed the fields, where he had harvested many crops. He glanced at his first schoolhouse. He took a final look at the graves of his father and brother. He left behind the first mine where he had worked. He wondered whether he was really exchanging lead for gold, or whether he might not gladly come back to Franklin County and again work in the lead mines. As he set out, lead seemed certain, dependable, within the touch of his hands; gold was glittering, fantastic, far away.

When Elizabeth Hearst went with her son on that last ride as he left for California, she wore her prettiest Leghorn bonnet, her cashmere shawl, for she had pretty things, and treasured them for great occasions. This was the greatest occasion of her life. The Hearsts rode out of the mining country into the vineyards of Gasconade County. It was like passing through a bit of France — the precise French vineyards, the pretty little gardens blossoming with spring flowers, the gay pink and white fruit trees in bloom, an occasional house of rock and masonry constructed with French grace and feeling. This old world charm and loveliness had an enchantment for Elizabeth Hearst, and for her son, who had an instinctive sense of beauty.

Elizabeth Hearst and Patsy rode for two days with George Hearst and Phillips. Not till the mother and daughter reached the ford of the Gasconade River could they bring themselves to turn homeward. When it came to the parting, speech left them. Years later, when George Hearst was rich and powerful, he confessed that when he said goodbye to to his mother and sister at the ford of the Gasconade, his determination melted. Ambition, California, El Dorados became nothing. He wished only to be with his mother and sister in their little log house on the plateau of the Ozarks. George Hearst waved his broad-brimmed hat in a signal of farewell. What would become of his loved ones? What would become of him? When he saw his mother and Patsy riding away from him, followed by the hounds with tails drooping, for a time he wished that there was no such thing as gold, and that he never had heard of California.

But soon he would come back, in a year or two, or three. He would make life easy for his mother and Patsy. They should see what he could do. They would be proud of him.

Ten days ahead of him on the trail were Cousin Joe and Cousin Jacob Clark, and the neighbors in the prairie schooners. Pride drove him on. He turned his horse westward.

# THE SEVENTH CHAPTER

H EARST and his companion, Phillips, followed the Ridge out of Missouri. The Ridge is a pleasant rolling upland that parallels the south bank of the Missouri to the western boundary of the state. It is clothed .in oak and sumach interspersed with bushy dells. The travelers did not touch the Missouri River. They went by Marysville, and the Gasconade, and kept the range all the way across to Kansas, then called the Indian Country.

Today the Ridge is dotted with towns, checkered with farms, and webbed with railways, but George Hearst's road in 1850 lay through widely scattered farms, huddles of houses called hamlets, and virgin forests. He and Phillips passed a little town that had made a gesture toward fame and had named itself Californiaville in its determination to have some of the glamor of the new Pacific Coast territory. Hearst and Phillips rode through Sedalia, then a crossroads town with one store. Hearst sent messages often to his mother. He realized that soon communication would be difficult.

He did not pass through Independence, Missouri, the

great outfitting center from which so many caravans had departed. Instead, he went to the south, and rode through the sunflower part of the Indian Country, now called Kansas. He found himself in the turmoil of the Santa Fé Trail. Whiskey, groceries, prints and notions were going to Santa Fé; and coming back were buffalo robes, dried beef, Indian blankets, pottery, turquoise, Mexican silver money, gold dust and silver bars. All blended were short-haired New Englanders, long-haired Missourians, singing Dons, painted Indians with serapes and silver belts, Indian sons from Taos, Acoma, Zuni, and "Oh, Suzanna." Here was the covered wagon world of adventurous America. George Hearst felt the spirit of it all, the thrill of the gold-seeker. It was the West as he had dreamed it, beautiful, unbound and barbaric. He wished to go farther. The eyes of this young man from the wild, log-cabin Missouri country gleamed as he thought of the plains ahead.

Hearst and Phillips planned to make twice the speed of the caravans and wagons in order to overtake Joe and Jacob Clark, and the others on the Big Blue. They hoped to join the caravans at night in order to have the protection of the corral of wagons.

George Hearst never forgot that first morning on the trail, when he became a part of the caravan. There were hustle and confusion around many little breakfast fires. Mothers were dressing their children. Women, not mothers, were watering geraniums, calla lilies and rose cuttings. Women tenderly put into the wagons hair-cloth chairs, wax flowers, canaries, Bibles. Then came the "jump-off." The loud "gees" and "haws," the prodding of the oxen. The great beasts leaped and bellowed. Hearst and Phillips urged forward their horses. Dogs barked madly. Chickens clucked in their coops. Women and children climbed into the ox-drawn wagons bound for California. Up and down the line roared the order: "Roll out! Roll out!"

A barefoot Missouri boy cracked his whip over the oxen. The train ground grimly over the road, cutting deep into the soil up to the hubs of the wheels. Hearst rode carelessly, rapidly, well. He was happy. His march to California and to fortune had begun.

The ox teams, slow-footed, low-headed, steady, indomitable, moved over a carpet of pink verbenas, blue larkspur, wild indigo, a magical carpet that would make all their dreams come true. There was singing, shouting, blowing of old bugles used in the Mexican War. Recklessness was in the air. They were moving away from civilization and about to enter the long trail to the far West. Suddenly all felt themselves plainsmen.

Hearst was glad he had come. The caravan would reach California before snowfall. Now Missouri seemed shut-in and tame. Here was lush spring life; watercress in the creeks; rivers filled with fish; wild turkeys mating; everywhere wild tulips, honeysuckle and lupines. What were difficulties to plainsmen? They could level the Rockies.

In their eagerness to reach California the great caravan broke line. Each tried to pass his neighbor. The leaders galloped back and forth reasoning, trying to restore order, cursing. What did they care about order, these eager pioneers who had a rendezvous with gold in California? They were living the fiery frontier life of the fifties.

It was a glorious experience for George Hearst to ride along the Kansas River toward the Big Blue, past groves of oak, hickory, dogwood and willows. He never ate such meals as these before the campfire, when he dined on wild onions and bacon and sang, "Oh, Suzanna." Sometimes the prairie schooners were stalled in the mud. Speedily they were hauled out, forward they went. Only two thousand more miles! Soon California—fairyland, where orange trees bloom in winter!

On the trail they met traders and trappers from Oregon, who tried to discourage them. California was no fairyland. In places it was cold. If they didn't hurry over the Sierra, they might freeze to death as had the Donners. The Oregonians urged them back. The trip would cut ten years from their lives. They might die of cholera. Turn back? Never! As one Missourian said: "No damn cholera could kill a man from Pike County!" On they went, gold-mad. Soon they would see buffaloes. Soon nuggets of gold would stick up out of the ground as large as your fist. The long, white serpent of covered wagons wound over the hills to the West along the Kansas River.

Indian villages were passed, and there were rumors that the Kiowa Indians would attack them with tomahawks. Hearst was not disturbed by rumors of Indian warfare. He had known red men from childhood. In Missouri and on the plains Hearst was friendly with Indians, perhaps because he had something of their simplicity. When the Kiowas finally came to speak to Hearst it was to tell him that they were hungry because all the game had been killed by trappers and immigrants. They brought him prairie potatoes, and he gave them jerked beef.

Not until the first storm came were the glamor and glitter of the California trail dimmed. It was a sombre prairie night. All the travelers were gathered around the campfire within their high wall of wagons. Dogs were barking. Coyotes wailed back their "Ya-ki-oo." Wolves howled hungrily. Owls hooted when the storm broke. The immigrants talked of cholera. Hundreds were dying on the trail. That first stormy night on the prairie was the loneliest of George Hearst's life. California seemed a mad chimera. Missouri was fairyland. There corn grew higher than a man's head. The memory of Missouri ham made him hungry. He thought of Gasconade County, with its beautiful vines; of Franklin County, with it comfortable cabins and charming uplands. If he had remained at home, perhaps he would have found a lead mine richer than La Motte. Was he running away from fortune?

Next morning was clear and bright. "Gee!" "Whoa!" "Haw!" Soon once more the immigrants moved westward. That day the caravans went fifteen miles over a rough prairie, the next day twelve, the third day twenty, the following day fourteen, the next day twenty-two. Hearst and Phillips more than doubled the speed of the first caravan. They were eager to join the Clarks and their neighbors on the Big Blue, but if possible they camped with the wagons. Frequently they had to help immigrants ford creeks.

At last, they reached the Kansas River ferry. Wagons were hauled by teams as close as possible to the boat-landing. Then they were lifted and pushed into boats by the united strength of men. Oxen, loose cattle and horses swam. Half-breed Indians ferried the people across. Hearst and Phillips rode fast toward the Big Blue. They passed several small water courses before they reached the Vermilion River, a rapid, racing river a quarter of a mile wide running between banks of oak and elm. At the Vermilion they were detained several hours. They helped a party of immigrants lower their wagons down by ropes, and by doubling teams hauled them to opposite banks. From the Vermilion to the Big Blue there was said to be no water nor wood. Hearst and Phillips filled their water casks and journeyed with the caravan in order to have fires at night and in the morning. They camped in a storm of thunder, rain and lightning which drenched them to the skin, but the sunset made a magnificent rainbow like an arc of triumph in the West.

Two days more, and they were at the Big Blue, a stream one hundred yards wide after the storm. The Big Blue was filled with driftwood, and they were obliged to delay several days. Hearst was disappointed that the Clarks and their neighbors had gone on ahead. He found a message in one of the trail post offices, a bit of paper attached to a split stake at the Big Blue ford: "We want to be in California before the snow. Don't delay. Please hurry." JOE CLARK.

The Big Blue was dangerously swollen, but the leaders were determined to risk crossing before it lowered to its normal depth. Someone had to swim the river to carry over the rope so that all might get across. For a long time no one ventured into the swift stream. Finally a little red-haired boy, carrying the rope, struck boldly out into the river. It was the courage of youth and inexperience. The immigrants standing on the shore breathlessly watched the dauntless red-haired boy land and wave his hand.

Hearst never forgot that red-haired boy. It seemed as if he had saved their lives by giving a week ahead of the Sierra storms they were seeking to avoid. Years later in Washington, when he was United States Senator, Hearst related the incident as a turning point in his career to the great wit, Colonel Tom Ochiltree of Texas, when they were dining at Chamberlain's. "I can see that red-headed boy yet, Colonel. I'd like to know where he is. If it hadn't been for him we might all have failed. If I could find him, I'd give him a hundred thousand dollars."

Ochiltree, the practiced joker, couldn't take even that remote tragic moment seriously. "Senator," he said, pretending to blush, "I remember the incident perfectly. I am that red-haired boy."

# THE EIGHTH CHAPTER

After they crossed the Big Blue, Hearst and Phillips rode through the Pawnee country. They themselves looked as black as Pawnees. Some of the spirit of gay adventure, with which they had set out, vanished on the journey. Among the poppies and lupines by the trail they began seeing graves of women, children, and even men, all marked with crude little wooden crosses and headstones. As they went on these stones seemed the milestones of cholera.

Hearst and Phillips rode faster, but no matter how fast they rode, nor with what hearty cheer they sang "Oh, Suzanna!" they were stalked by the memory of those sleeping on the prairie. Hearst realized that like him those Argonauts had set out for California with youth, strength and determination to conquer, but those stark headstones marked what was left of them. Cholera defied courage, strength, ambition, youth.

In 1841 the cholera pestilence swept out of the East. It devastated India, China, Arabia, Turkey, Egypt, North Africa. In 1847 it entered Europe by way of Russia and

Germany, spread through England and France. In 1849 it made its appearance among the gold-seekers. Like the wolves, it lurked on the flanks of the immigrants, ravaging their ranks. In that summer of 1850 it was in every camp, striking down the strongest. When Hearst and Phillips saw the graves increase, they shuddered, and rode faster. But always when Hearst had an opportunity he sent back a cheerful message to his mother and Patsy.

Hearst purchased of the Indians dried buffalo tongue and jerked beef, which he and his companion packed in skins on their horses. In the distance, but beyond rifle range, they saw wild turkeys, panthers, elks. The great sight was antelopes grazing at a distance of two or three miles. Stealthily Hearst and Phillips tried to come upon the antelopes, but the animals sensed them at half a mile. The animals' small sinewy limbs carried them away with the fleetness of birds.

A few days after crossing the Big Blue, Hearst and Phillips camped on the bank of the Little Blue. They rode along this river, ascending over bluffs into a high tableland in order to strike the Platte River, twenty-seven miles away. They camped opposite Grand Island, where the Platte was about four hundred and fifty feet wide, but slow, sluggish, turgid. Here the trail followed the broad, flat bottom lands on the south bank in a sweeping curve downward to new Fort Kearney. Hearst and Phillips longed to reach new Fort Kearney. They hoped that there they would overtake the Clarks. Hearst hungered for the sight of the adobe walls of the fort. He spoke of the flour and bacon they would buy when they reached the fort. Hearst and Phillips had come three hundred and fifty miles on horseback. In their eagerness to over-

take their friends they had not slept, nor had they eaten
sufficiently. Could Elizabeth Hearst have seen her son
she would have known that her mother heart had made
no mistake. George Hearst was nearly thirty, but he was
only her boy. He needed her care and food. He was
worn-out, exhausted.

At last Hearst and his companion reached Fort Kearney. The fort was overcrowded; no bed for these young
gold-seekers. On the open prairie, outside the walls,
they crawled between their blankets and slept. Before
dawn a tremendous storm beat down, drenching their
shivering bodies. Hearst and Phillips rose and went on
in the rain.

This rain continued for twenty-one days; but rain and
wind and storm could not drive George Hearst back to
safety and shelter in the fort. He was of the persecuted
Scotch Covenanters, and of the frontier of Missouri.
Twenty-one days of rain could not break his will, even
though in the storm always more graves marked the trail.
Each grave warned him of the price that men pay for
adventure and security from poverty. The harder it
poured, the wilder the wind blew across the prairies, the
more resolute he was not to turn back from California,
even though the pestilence of cholera was sweeping the
trail in an invisible cyclone.

Ahead of Hearst and Phillips was a family from Indiana. One day the old father and mother of the party
turned back their teams. They had buried their five sons
on the prairie; all they had in the world. They told Hearst
they themselves had not cared for gold. They had taken
the journey to be with their boys. Now they were going
back to Indiana alone. For a time they remained with

Hearst and Phillips, baring their grief. Then they set out for their home.

Still George Hearst went on. Then in the midst of a terrible downpour on Plum Creek, he had a chill. He had never felt a chill like this. He knew what it meant. It was the first symptoms of cholera. Then followed thirst, stomach pains, cramped legs, diarrhea. His features were pinched, his eyes sunken. He was in such pain that he could not speak aloud to Phillips. In the midst of that long, ceaseless twenty-one day downpour he lay powerless. In after life he never forgot that cruel bed in grass six feet high, a grass grave. From the bottom of his soul he longed to lie there forever. Hearst recalled that he had some brandy, for which he had paid sixteen dollars a gallon in St. Louis, and some pills given him by a friend. He gulped the pills and drank the brandy feverishly, trying to still his consciousness. He wondered how long he could live. He thought it strange that he had made all this effort to be buried on an Indian Country prairie in a storm, like those five young gold-seekers from Indiana. As he lay in the grass recalling Missouri, with its beautiful vines, its mines, and his mother and sister in their cabin, he heard a distant voice in a caravan singing, "Old Grimes is Dead, That Old Man."

But death was not to call for George Hearst in the Indian Country. Life and destiny had too much to offer. In twenty-four hours the alarming cholera symptoms were arrested. His pulse grew stronger. His body regained its warmth and natural hue. The acute danger passed. A few days of weakness, and he was better. He rode forward on the Overland Trail.

# THE NINTH CHAPTER

Hearst and Phillips tried to make up for the time lost by illness. They hurried through the great valley of the Platte, the highway to the Rockies. The soil was sandy. There were a hundred varieties of wild grasses. Mosquitoes were maddening. They rode up the Platte until the river was two miles wide and as impressive as the Missouri or Mississippi. Frequently they met trappers floating down the Platte, which often could be waded, so shallow was the water. These trappers were usually bound for John Jacob Astor's St. Louis trading post. At times the trappers got out of their boats to push them off the shallows.

Occasionally Hearst had a note from the Clarks and the wagons ahead. He found one fastened to the skull of a buffalo. The ground was strewn with buffalo bones. Often he saw buffalo wallows, impressions big as a circus ring and ten or twelve feet deep, where bulls lashed and rolled in a welter of mud and fury. Hearst never forgot the first black herd of buffalo that he saw plunge down to the platte, making the ground tremble as if from an earthquake.

Early in July Hearst crossed the south fork of the Platte, and saw buffalo in herds of five hundred to a thousand on the plains to the south. After the travelers crossed the Platte, the buffalo herds increased, but the buffaloes were difficult to kill. A giant buffalo could carry twenty bullets and still run.

After Hearst passed over the prairies to the north fork of the Platte the earth grew more barren. Blue lupines were everywhere, but no shrubs or trees were visible. Hearst and Phillips increased their speed. They felt gladly certain that soon they must overtake the Clarks and their wagons.

At last they came to a spring of pure water, surrounded by wild currants and gooseberries, at the entrance to a dry ravine where there were a few ash trees: Ash Hollow. Here was a log cabin, and improvised post office, where letters were sent to every part of the earth. Near the post office were camped Joe Clark and his party. Hearst and Cousin Joe rushed together with whoops of joy.

For the first time since Hearst and Phillips set out, they had a meal cooked by women, with wild honey, dried buffalo, and prairie potatoes. There were even hot biscuits baked in a Dutch oven set in the ashes of the campfire. The travelers celebrated by buying milk from some immigrants who were driving their own cows to California. That supper took Hearst back to Franklin County. Missouri seemed very near, and California far away.

Now that Hearst had joined his relatives and friends, he had a new impetus in going from Ash Hollow. They were only a hundred and fifty miles from Fort Laramie, but they went slowly, because the wagon wheels sank ten inches into the sand of the arid, desolate plain. At every step they inhaled gray dust.

On this road Hearst always recalled that they overtook two nice looking young fellows with a spanking team of oxen. These boys killed a buffalo heifer, which they shared with the Hearst party. They were about to drive on with their spanking team, when one of the boys said he was very thirsty. Would Hearst ask his partner to handle the oxen while he went for water. Hearst recognized the sign of cholera. The boy died two days later.

Tragedy was everywhere among animals as among men. Cows were broken by the strain, oxen died, crippled horses were shot. Many of the animals that bore the burdens to California must have felt as they panted forward, tongues lolling, that life not death was the tragedy of the trail; but bravely they went on under creaking loads.

On the Fourth of July, when Hearst and his friends were toiling toward Fort Laramie, they stopped at noon, ate buffalo meat, drank some St. Louis brandy, fired off guns, and sang the national anthem. Then they went on.

Thirty or forty miles distant was Chimney Rock, visible to the immigrants. Court House Rock, looking like the Capitol at Washington, stood out majestically. Twenty miles farther Hearst saw Scott's Bluff, a large isolated pile of sandstone curiously carved by the weather into minarets, domes, temples, Gothic castles. As the travelers approached Scott's Bluff, the trail left the river. They passed through a smooth valley of seven or eight miles in the rear of the bluffs. They began to climb upwards. At three in the afternoon they had their first view of the peaks of the Rocky Mountains. One hundred and fifty miles away was Laramie's Peak, and farther on the more distant Wind River Mountains with their summits like small white clouds. In a storm Hearst went down the ridge through a barren country with deep chasms and ravines, then over the plain to the Platte. In a hurly-burly of thunder, lightning and 'wind the party encamped, still in a storm. It was like sleeping in a river. Just before sunset, with rain pouring, thunder rumbling, lightning flashing, they arrived at Fort Laramie. For the first time since leaving home they saw the American flag flying.

Three thousand Sioux Indians were encamped on the plain surrounding the fort. An immense number of Indian horses were grazing on the plains. The Sioux had gathered to organize a war party to attack Snakes and Crows. Many of them were intoxicated, including some of the lovely light copper Sioux women. Outside the fort the Indians danced wildly, and sang their songs.

Fort Laramie, or Fort John as it was sometimes called, was a large adobe quadrangle stockade on Laramie River near where it joins the Platte, on a barren plain. Indians were allowed to enter the fort during the day, but at night they slept on the plain. Several immigrant trains were camping there, engaged in trading. It was the chief trading post of the American Fur Company. A party of Sioux Indians rode in from a victorious expedition against the Pawnees, bringing with them twenty-five scalps and many horses.

While they camped at Fort Laramie and laid in supplies, Hearst and his friends talked with many on their way east from California. All were disgruntled. They had lived there four years, and it hadn't rained in all that time. Not only was it not a decent place in which to live, but they didn't believe there was gold in California.

But there was no turning back now. The travelers

toiled on up the barren Rocky Mountains in a deathlike torpor and silence. Even greasewood, sage, sunflowers and wild daisies were perishing under the hot sun in the sand impregnated with sulphur, alkali and salt. The travelers sighted a small stream of water, and eagerly rushed to it; the water was bitter with salt and alkali. In the lower end of the valley, in the side of a bank, they finally found some pure water. They filled their casks, and went on up to Independence Rock. Here were masses of rock a mile or more in circumference. Thousands of names of those who had passed this way were written or graven on this rock. But Hearst did not write his name there.

Hearst's caravan passed through the Sweetwater Valley and crossed the river. Always it seemed to Hearst that most of the two thousand miles between Missouri and California consisted of rivers; clear rivers, muddy rivers, hot rivers, icy rivers, swift rivers, sluggish rivers, rocky rivers, quicksand rivers, shallow rivers with hidden obstructions, rivers swollen by cloudbursts, rivers poisoned by alkali, rivers to be approached through swamps, rivers to be tumbled into from precipices. Each river was a threat of death. All these rivers had to be conquered. Small wonder that a popular song of the trail was "One More River to Cross." Hearst came to hate rivers. He longed for the desert.

After Hearst and his friends crossed the Sweetwater River they were scarcely conscious of it, but they were ascending the ridge separating the waters of the Atlantic from the Pacific. They stood on the backbone of the American continent. They took their last look at the Atlantic side. Now they were in the West, the real West.

For Hearst there was an exhilaration in this bold, free

life. The indelible impression made upon him by those months in the open was never erased. Always he demanded something larger, freer, than so-called civilization offered.

Every kind of success came to him, but he could not be wholly bound by an artificial life. Never was any house so wonderful to him as the sky when he stood on the backbone of America. Nothing so satisfied his being as the Rockies. No matter how exquisite was the furniture, nor how rare, no bed was ever so soft as a blanket on the ground. The trail got into his blood. To the end he was always the man of the plains and the mountains.

# THE TENTH CHAPTER

HEARST and his friends made straight for Fort Bridger. At this great height the view was sublime. In a barren, inhospitable wilderness of sand and clay, with dead-brown vegetation, they forded Green River, the head of the Colorado, which ran swiftly down through the cottonwood and willow trees. In hot August they saw lofty snowy crests of the Utah Mountains. Above the travelers impended rocks of sand and clay, below them were chasms. The only beauty was an occasional mirage. One blistering August day, when they dropped down from a butte into the valley where lay Fort Bridger, it seemed Paradise. Two or three log cabins nestled in clumps of cottonwood on a flat near a small stream filled with mountain trout. This was Fort Bridger, with Jim Bridger as host.

All the West had heard of Jim Bridger, hunter, trapper, scout, guide. He was almost as well-known as the Rocky Mountains. He came and went, but no one ever knew his real name. He was called the "king of mountain men." Twenty-five years before he had discovered Great Salt

Lake. He had been host to all the West. With equal friendliness and rough grace he entertained Indians, Mormons, Missourians, trappers from the Rockies and tráders from Taos. He could not write his name, but knew these Rockies like a Shoshone chief, and he looked the character. A tall, spare man with long, dank hair, gray stubble beard, shrewd eyes peering out from bushy brows under a low, wide hat. He rode an Indian pad-saddle without stirrups. His fringed shirt, leggings and moccasins of skin made him look what he was—the oldest scout of the Rockies. He had two squaw wives, numerous half-breed children and a friendly thirst. His stories of the trail went from the Atlantic to the Pacific. Near Bridger's five hundred Sioux Indians were en-camped. At Bridger's dry goods, groceries, tobacco and ammunition could be obtained, also milk for ten cents a quart and whiskey for two dollars a pint. Hearst laid in fresh supplies and acquired Bridger's knowledge of the road.

At Bridger's Hearst was met by a plausible Mormon bent on cultivating cordial relations with Californians. The Mormon tried to persuade them to go by a shorter route around the southern end of the Great Salt Lake and pass through Salt Lake City, the new metropolis of the Latter Day Saints. The Mormon publicity man did not say that Latter Day Saints charged twenty-five dollars for a hundred pounds of flour, and for other things in pro-portion. Jim Bridger quietly advised George Hearst against the southern route with its ninety miles of desert that had brought death and disaster to the Donner party. Kindly destiny guiding Hearst, and his own excellent judgment, took him by the northern, a longer but safer route by way of the Humboldt River.

There was a light shower as the Hearst party ascended from the valley, and this freshened the wild sage growth of the mountains. The quivering aspen poplars in the hollows were a brighter green. On the hot dusty way it made the travelers seem cooler when they noticed there was a fresh fall of snow on the mountains.

Beyond Bridger's the Overland Trail always took a heavy toll of life. Everywhere were bleaching bones of oxen and horses. Wagons and farming utensils were abandoned by Oregonians who suddenly succumbed to the California gold excitement. The Hearst party encouraged themselves by saying that soon they would be in California. The whips cracked more loudly. The tired animals quickened their pace. Even the oxen seemed to know they were near the end of the journey.

Hearst and his friends entered what is now Utah—then the Mormon state of Deseret—through Echo Canyon, a Gothic-like gorge of the Wasatch Mountains, over a wagon road built by Brigham Young. One evening in the distance as the sun was sinking Hearst first saw Great Salt Lake, a sea of pale scarlet fire. In the south and west rose masses of metallic looking mountains.

From that time until they reached the desert the Hearst party largely followed the trail of John C. Fremont. They struck camp in a narrow mountain gorge. At half past one the next morning they rose in order to cross the desert in one day, and to avoid the hazard of camping there at night. They must not lose their mules and oxen and horses as did the Donner party in 1846. They determined to eat only bread; bacon excited too much thirst. They filled a powder-keg with coffee, and barrels with water. All they had to do was to hurry due west.

The travelers had their coffee and bread early. As

soon as the light broke they began their march over the great salt plain which was like a sepulchre. Whipped by terror they went at full speed across the flat of alkali and sagebrush with its horned toads and rattlesnakes, its ashy, snowy sand, and its white clouds of dust. As the heat beat down upon them it seemed an inferno of a crazed imagination. At times the desert sand resembled waving water inundating them in billows. They crossed beds of dead salt lakes. The wind blew the salt toward them. They breathed salt, tasted salt. Even the mules hesitated; tried to countermarch. Again Hearst asked himself what made him leave Missouri for California? Why couldn't he have been sensible and remained where he was born? The women fell asleep as they traveled. The cattle drowsed as they stumbled onward. The men almost slept as they walked, ox-goads in hand, over unreal, strange earth.

Suddenly there were trees, villas, palaces, water, fountains. Caravans were coming toward them. Hearst saw his own image hastening toward him. Then he knew that the beauty was only a mirage. They were jeered at by ghost caravans in the desert, "Gee!" "Whoa!" "Haw!"

There was only one escape from it all. Speed! No matter whether they ate or drank they must keep up that terrible speed.

At last, through clouds of salty sand, dimly they saw the mountains for which they were heading. As darkness came on the mountains were their sole guide. Lights blazed from the mountain side. The Snake Indians were lending generous aid to strange wayfarers of the white race. The moon came out, and Hearst and his party kept on going by the Indians' signal until about nine o'clock that night. They stumbled through grass, sage, willows, and discovered a faint trickle of water. Men, mules, oxen, horses rushed into the stream and thirstily gulped together of its muddy waters. Later among the reeds and willows they discovered a spring.

# THE ELEVENTH CHAPTER

H EARST and his friends had been tested by heat, cold, rain and desert. They survived, and they felt immune to illness. Exposure sought out the weak spots in their constitutions. As they crossed Utah toward St. Mary's River, now the Humboldt, they made their way through a blazing flat of alkali and sagebrush. The Humboldt was a joy for the travelers, with its pleasant, grassy valley and willows along the stream. There were more valleys, and more valleys, all separated by ridges. As the trail ran west water became scarcer. The salt and alkali waste, clothed with mesquite, lay broiling in the mid-summer desert heat. By this time it seemed that they had been to California and back several times, but El Dorado always receded on the horizon.

To make matters worse, one of the men of the Hearst party was stricken with measles. He was so weakened by the hardships of the trail that he could go no farther. At first it did not seem serious, but death always moved with the caravan. Like the other travelers the Hearst party had their lonely burial rites, and one more headstone marked the Overland Trail. Hearst went south along the Humboldt River from what is now Winnemucca to the Humboldt Sink, taking the route later followed by the Central Pacific Railroad. Then another blow: one of the travelers was stricken with paralysis. He became an additional charge, but he was brought through to California.

After the Humboldt River disappeared beneath the sands of the Sink, fewer were the oxen, fewer the horses, fewer the men. Deception Valley, Destruction Flat, Mirage—these names told the story of this hell-hole of the desert. Beasts were too weak to support anything but their own diminished weight. Men went mad. The stench from dead animals beside the trail was sickening. Buzzards hovered overhead waiting to prey on the fallen. Men fled from their wagons in their feverish eagerness to reach the water of the Carson River. That year three million dollars worth of property was abandoned on this desert.

At this crucial stage, George Hearst felt like one of the poor dumb brutes. As he was beaten down in the fierce desert heat, like the dying oxen, his tongue was swollen. As men and animals moaned and groaned, he wondered why someone wasn't kind enough to end the misery of them all. This was worse than the cholera. In fact, it was one of the results of cholera. Never could Hearst outgrow the memory of that Nevada illness. Only on rare occasions in after life could he be induced to discuss this part of the journey.

After Hearst recovered sufficiently to travel, the party followed the trail, passed the Carson Sink and reached the blessed river. At last good water and good grass for the surviving beasts. Here, too, was Ragtown, built of abandoned tents, abandoned hopes, wagon covers, the misery and rags of the trail. Traders sold supplies at the flat rate of one dollar a pound. They stripped the immigrants not only of their money but of their watches, rings and pins, and their worn-out stock. Many of the pioneers made the rest of the way on foot. George Hearst left the last of his money in Ragtown. He paid one hundred dollars for a sack of flour. But he still had his five franc piece given him by the French miners when he was a little boy.

Along the Carson River, about every twenty miles, were relief stations financed by generous business men in San Francisco and Sacramento. If an immigrant was entirely destitute, he was given a pint of flour and a pint of corn meal. With grim humor George Hearst said that at least he did not have to go to relief stations; he had left his five franc piece. But he had no fear. Over the granite crest of the Sierra was El Dorado.

The travelers passed Mormon Station—now Genoa—near Carson City. The road ran up the river to Carson Pass, crossing the stream six times before it emerged at the eastern foot of the Sierra Nevada. They must scale the summit that stood before them like a great, gray fortress. Here was the steepest and roughest part of the entire Overland route. Men grew in moral stamina as they conquered each mile of that narrow road. In places there was barely room for a wagon to pass between vertical rocks rising three or four hundred feet. In other places the wagon crawled up and down solid smooth cliffs almost perpendicular for several yards. Then they crashed into mud holes. Hearst and the Clarks agreed that it was the worst road ever traveled by man. But others had passed, and so would they.

When George Hearst reached the summit he took off his hat to the giant pine trees, to the mountains, to the blue sky. He breathed deep and full the incense of the forest. He felt as if he had conquered the world. Once more he was a Scotch Presbyterian. In silence he gave thanks. At last, California!

# THE TWELFTH CHAPTER

H EARST and his party toiled and sweated to the South
Fork of the American River, that magical river where
James Marshall first saw the shimmer that dazzled him
and made the world drunk with desire for gold. When
George Hearst came to this stream, high up in the pine-
covered mountains, he felt its enchantment and lure.
With new momentum he hastened over the snow-covered
Second Summit, passed Two Lakes, Leek Springs,
Traders' Creek and came to the Junction.

At the Junction the travelers followed the right fork
of the road toward Hangtown. Almost gaily they went
along the ridge between the South Fork of Weber Creek
and the North Fork of the Cosumnes River. It was October, 1850. Six months before they had left Missouri, and
their worst troubles were over. It seemed a symbol of
their journey that they first paused to rest in Pleasant
Valley.

This valley was a park-like stretch for several miles on
either side of Clear Creek. Here were fir trees and white
oaks, with quail fluttering and whirring. The settlement

consisted of a log hotel, a blacksmith shop, a store and a saloon, but to Hearst weakened by cholera, fever, and and six months of rough travel, it was a California paradise. Hearst and his friends halted for rest. After the long straining weariness came the joy of doing nothing, of sleeping, then sleeping again, then eating quail and hot corn bread in the warm, beautiful California October Indian summer. Pleasant Valley was filled with camping gold-seekers, Mexicans, Chileans and a few Americans. In the Hearst party were four women with their husbands. As a rule, not more than one percent of the gold-seekers were women, and so these women attracted almost as much attention as a new strike.

Hearst could not remain long in Pleasant Valley. He was greatly refreshed by the happy delay, but there was no deep rest for him, listening as he did day and night to the living romantic dramas of the mines. He saw displayed real nuggets, sacks of dust. He thrilled to the news of the discovery. He must press forward, share the excitement of the diggings, be a part of that life of El Dorado which he neared. The very names beckoned to Hearst, each with a tale of a rich strike: Condemned Bar, Horseshoe Bar, Whiskey Bar, Spanish Dry Diggings, Volcano Bar, Dead Man's Bar, Milkpunch Bar, Rattlesnake Bar, Wildcat Bar, and Growlersburg. These were among the richest diggings. Then there was Hangtown, only a few months old, but with several thousand population. Beyond was Coloma, where Marshall himself lived. These tented cities on the hills and in the ravines summoned Hearst. Their fortunes would be his fortunes. Marshall, the discoverer, once lived in Missouri. Hearst was a practical miner. Why should he not be another Marshall?

But where were the rich diggings to make him a Marshall? Hearst and his party went on toward the bustling, roaring, gold-crazy camps. Before Hearst reached Diamond Springs, three miles from Hangtown, the report came that across the river from Murderer's Bar was the Big Crevice out of which J. D. Galbraith and three others, working three hours a day for eight days, had taken out forty-six hundred dollars.

After a few miles' journey through the valley, down the road and slope, they reached Diamond Springs, a pleasant mineral spring resort. Later it had several thousand population, but at this time it was only a small mining camp with a few wild, young, red-shirted, unshorn workmen, all drunk on dreams of finding the Great Mother Lode sprawled under these mountains, the pure gold source from which came the mesmeric nuggets in the gravel of the streams. At Diamond Springs, Hearst met Missourians. Already thousands were in California. They gave him a friendly welcome, but he was bewildered by their contradictory enthusiasms and advice.

After a short time in Diamond Springs, Hearst went on to Hangtown. This gold metropolis was only a year and a half old, but already it had possessed three names: Ravine City, then Old Dry Diggings, and last Hangtown. Expressive Hangtown had been recently well christened. Two Mexicans and an American robbed a miner. Swift, primitive, ruthless revenge followed. From a great oak on Main Street were hung the Mexicans and the American. When Hearst arrived in Hangtown the old oak with its benevolent arms extending over the street was proudly pointed out to him as a symbol of justice.

Hangtown was the metropolis of El Dorado County and very self-conscious. It was situated between the

South Fork of the American River and the North Fork of the Cosumnes. All the immigrants from the Carson River trail bound for Sacramento and San Francisco stopped here. Hangtown was one of the largest communities in California. Its voting strength was greater than that of all El Dorado County today. Day and night the immigrant ravine road leading into town was lined with prairie schooners filled with gold-seekers and freight wagons of the carriers. Already the town was headquarters for several stage lines, one going to Sacramento. Later Hank Monk, "Curly" Dan Burch, "Coon-Hollow Charlie," and other picturesque stage drivers, famous all over the West, were to make Hangtown their headquarters.

When Hearst reached Hangtown, the diggings felt grand, indeed. It had a real brick building more than a year old. It had a theatre. Father Ingoldsby had established a Roman Catholic Church, and the Reverend Jacob Speck had founded a Methodist Church. Abe and Rudolph Seligman supplied fashionable men's apparel, just like New York—some said better. Rudolph Seligman was later to be the New York and London banker. In Hines' blacksmith and wagon shop a seventeen year old boy named Studebaker was turning out miners' wheelbarrows. Today his name is on automobiles. Stephen T. Gage, later vice-president of the Central Pacific Railroad, had a pack-train freighting goods from the Carson River to Hangtown. Hangtown Creek had yielded a million dollars. In the rear of Tom Ashton's Round Tent Saloon and gambling house Mr. Wiley had washed out thirteen hundred dollars worth of "color" from one pan of white clay. Express offices and banks were bursting with nuggets. Hangtown was flush with gold.

George Hearst had only a five franc piece, his strength, his youth, high hopes, but he borrowed from his friends and mingled in the crowd of young Mexicans, Chileans, Chinese, Sydney "coves," Irish, English, French, Germans, Italians, Scandinavians, New Yorkers, New Englanders, Southerners, Missourians that milled through the narrow, twisted, tented streets exchanging tales of the greatest new strike, intoxicating each other by their words, exultant with the vision of the nebulous riches of the future. Like the other gold-seekers, George Hearst felt himself a millionaire.

But he indulged in none of the fantastic luxuries of the diggings' millionaire. He did not go to Emigrant Jane's Fandango House, nor to the Boomerang Saloon, nor to El Dorado Hotel, where bean soup was a dollar; tame beef from Arkansas (prime cut) one dollar and a half; baked beans (plain) seventy-five cents, (greased) one dollar; hash (low grade) seventy-five cents, (eighteen-carat) one dollar; codfish balls (per pair) seventy-five cents; rice pudding with brandy peaches two dollars; prunes seventy-five cents; one potato one dollar and twenty-five cents. All this was "payable in advance— gold scales on end of bar." No feasting for George Hearst and his friends in Hangtown.

Hearst quietly observed everything, went into the gulches and studied the conformation of the ground, asked questions. He found out that there were no more desirable claims to be had in the Coloma district, and so he decided to return to Diamond Springs.

Just as Hearst set out Hangtown had a spasm of "cleaning up." All the scarlet ladies in the town were escorted, with the band, to Sacramento Hill, and warned not to return. Later these same ladies did return, but to nurse Hangtown stricken with smallpox.

Another incident happened to make Hearst glad to leave Hangtown. Dick Crone, an Irish boy, had dealt monte at El Dorado Saloon. He thought he detected a player cheating. So he killed him with one upward plunge of a knife. Vigilantes quickly gathered to hang Dick Crone to the great oak tree of justice and equality, but a man was ill at Herrick's Hotel near the oak. The sick man was not disturbed. "Irish Dick" was lariated and strung up to another tree.

To be in Diamond Springs seemed to Hearst like being in his own home state, Missouri, so many Missourians were there. He wandered into ravines and over surrounding hills with a fellow Missourian. From the top of a high hill this man pointed out where gold was being washed out thirteen miles farther to the south. This was called Jackass Gulch, so named because of the accidental shooting of a jackass which had been mistaken by some miners for a grizzly bear.

Hearst and the Clarks went back to Pleasant Valley and then sweated their way over a dusty, dry trail, up and down the red-yellow hills with rocks jutting out of the surface between dusty manzanita shrubs. They finally reached Jackass Gulch, wooded with fir and oak, and flaming with poison oak crimsoned by early frost. That first night in Jackass Gulch they flung themselves down, wrapped themselves in their blankets and slept soundly on a bed of pebbles.

# THE THIRTEENTH CHAPTER

GEORGE HEARST was well equipped for the life of a California gold-seeker. He was thirty years of age, and in his whole existence he had never known an easy or soft day. For him life was one unending test of endurance. After he and his cousins, the Clarks, established themselves in Jackass Gulch, El Dorado County, on the North Fork of the Cosumnes River, he needed this stable, sturdy foundation of heredity and youth. These young pioneers dreamed toilsome dreams. They had to split the rocky land for gold. In Jackass Gulch was no roaring excitement, no roistering, no gay fandango houses—only hard work from early in the morning until late at night.

Joe Clark immediately began building the winter cabin. Hearst prospected, shoveled dirt and washed it. All the while he was storing up knowledge of placer mining. Sometimes he got nothing. Sometimes he found nuggets of two or three dollars. Then he felt jubilant, rich. He dreamed of finding a huge nugget, one gorgeous enough to send to his mother and to his sister, Patsy. Finally he discovered a nugget worth nineteen dollars.

That night he scarcely slept. The next day he worked faster. He explored every crevice for the purest gold.

Cousin Joe Clark, six years younger than George Hearst, was the life of the gulch. He was always the dandy, gay, happy, full of laughter and pranks. He declared he was the only one in the gulch who cared whether the cabin was tidied up or minded whether lizards nested in the blankets. He was an epicure and host for the Hearst-Clark cabin. Each took his turn at cooking. Suppers were usually salt pork and beans, with occasionally a jack rabbit or quail and tea or coffee. On rare occasions they had chops or steak. They usually had salaratus bread, or flapjacks made of water, flour, with a pinch of salt mixed in, all fried in grease. Sunday was set aside for mending and making bread for the week.

One day Cousin Joe Clark, with great gusto, promised them a treat—gingerbread. When the gingerbread was baked, it was found that he had used mustard instead of ginger. He gave them a glorious Christmas dinner, venison, a bottle of old Monongahela, a potpie topped with taffy-pulling. When New Year's day came, they all took plates, knives, and forks, and went to a cabin up the canyon and feasted on a grizzly, with potatoes, and the stuff that makes people happy for a short time.

During the entire winter, in all kinds of weather, George Hearst stood in the yellow mud, grimly shoveling gravel into the cradle or long Tom. His is no tale of easy, sudden success. So little was his gain that sometimes he said Jackass Gulch was well-named. After a few weeks' work, when they made their "clean-up," George Hearst knew that he and the Clarks would never be millionaires by washing gold in that unyielding granite canyon. The dust simply wasn't there. Already prospectors were scattering. Every day new strikes were being made else-where. Just beyond there were always millions—like a luring mirage. Gold Hill, at Grass Valley, was the new mesmeric word that passed from mining camp to mining camp, from gulch to gulch, from canyon to canyon, from mountain top to mountain top. At last the Mother Lode had been discovered!

That first year Hearst didn't think much of placer mining. In truth, he had little luck with his placer claims. After Hearst and the Clarks paid their winter expenses, bought some new mining equipment, supplied themselves with good mustangs and saddles, Hearst found that he had forty dollars in his pocket in dust. He was glad to hasten to the new Northern Mines, in what was later called the Bret Harte Country. He set out for Grass Valley and Nevada City.

It was early California spring. Grass was six inches high. They wound over the mountain, riding on a carpet of wild flowers. Hearst had a great love of land. He saw California at its most beautiful moment. He felt sure that wheat and fruit would grow in the valleys, and that California was destined to be a rich and powerful state.

In Grass Valley again Hearst was among Missouri friends. The first permanent settler of this place was Jules Rosiere, a French miner from Washington County, Missouri. Rosiere came over the immigrant trail in 1849. On Deer Creek his cattle strayed from their camp. They were found contentedly feeding and fattening on the tall, juicy grass on the banks of Wolf Creek. Rosiere decided to remain there, and so the place was called Grass Valley. Since 1849 Hangtown miners had "creviced" with rich success on Wolf Creek. By the summer of 1849 the whole region was being explored for gold. In 1850 there was a slump. The miners scattered to other camps.

But in October 1850, the very month of Hearst's arrival at Pleasant Valley, a man named McKnight discovered an elbow of the Mother Lode, shining and brilliant, the source of all the gold of the Sierra Nevada. This discovery was named Gold Hill, and Grass Valley was born again. Then began the deepest mining the world has ever known.

Gold Hill was so rich that it frightened miners. Some declared there was little of the white quartz; it was a mountain of solid gold. Gold Hill made miners fear that gold would be demonetized and become as common as lead. Later it was discovered that the ledge in Gold Hill was two feet wide. This news drove miners wild. Hills were filled with prospectors. Other camps were deserted. Hearst had a "lucky" feeling when he arrived in Grass Valley.

A few miles away another mining camp had sprung up, Nevada City, situated at the entrance to Deer Creek. In 1848 James Marshall had mined there without success, but already Nevada City had become another Hangtown. In 1851 it was larger than Sacramento, and one of the most important settlements in the state. It had two hundred and fifty buildings, scores of tents and cabins spreading over surrounding hills for a radius of more than two miles. Five thousand people had arrived from Sacramento, and were living in tents. Hundreds were hurrying up the river from San Francisco. The banks of the Sacramento River were heaped with goods and provisions for the mines. Wages were eight dollars a day, but few men would work for wages. Huge nuggets were tossed about. At every turn were gambling houses.

Nevada City had little law, but lots of order. Men were flogged for stealing. Nevada City declared it had the cheapest justice in the state.

One of the first things Hearst saw in Nevada City was a specimen as large as a man's head, brought from Grass Valley, and exhibited in Hamlet Davis' store on Broad Street. This quartz was white stone, and had solid streaks of gold worked in. It was supposed to be worth six thousand dollars. To add thrill to the excitement two miners came in with a pack load of ore from the North Fork of the Yuba River, the result of two months' work. This load assayed forty-three thousand dollars.

Hearst and the Clarks went out prospecting with some success. Immediately they turned over their claims. There was no doubt about it, Nevada City bore quicker returns than Jackass Gulch. George Hearst was always casual and modest in recounting the various steps of his fortune. But Charles D. Ferguson in his *A Third of a Century In The Gold Fields*, and also Thompson and West, historians of Nevada County, indicate that in 1851 Hearst became part owner in the first theatre in Nevada City, and this was the finest theatre on the Mother Lode. They recorded that this theatre was the old Dramatic Hall, on the northeast corner of Broad and Pine Streets, over the store of Davis and Hearst. Thompson and West wrote that: "These gentlemen had a reading room in the second story of their building which was supplied by papers from all over the world uncalled for at the Sacramento post office." Thousands of papers were turned over by the Sacramento post office to Davis and Hearst. In order to make room for the theatre, an addition was built at the end of the reading room. The joists were extended over Pine Street, and room was made for the wings of the stage. The theatre opened in 1851. The actors were Doctor and Mrs. Robinson, Mrs. Mestayer and Tench S. Fairchild. Doctor Robinson was celebrated for his Yankee stories, told in the name of Hezekiah Pickerill. The first play given was *Christopher Strap*. Soon the *Lady of Lyons* was on the boards, Mrs. Robinson taking the role of the lady, and a young man named Edwards that of Claude Melnotte.

The miners were delighted. There was great rivalry to see who could applaud his favorite most noisily. Theatrical performances were given in this theatre until 1854. It was the only theatre in Nevada City until 1854, with the exception of the Jenny Lind, erected as a rival in 1851.

The Jenny Lind had a short life and a befitting tragic dramatic end. During a storm in March 1852, Deer Creek was filled with logs and driftwood. Bridges were carried away. A heavy log struck the Main Street bridge, ripped it from its foundation, sweeping away the props that sustained the theatre. "There she goes!" cried Nevada City, as the building swayed and toppled into the stream. This disaster left the Davis-Hearst theatre supreme.

Among those who appeared at this theatre were the Robinson family, the Chapman family, Mr. Wallach, Edwin Booth, Julia Dean Hayne, Mr. and Mrs. Stark, Kate Hayes, the Alleghanians and Estelle Porter. Bayard Taylor lectured there.

Doubtless in this theatre many times sat Lola Montez, the dancer, who came to Grass Valley at this period, after having upset the throne of King Ludwig of Bavaria. Here, too, was Madame Moustache, the handsome bejeweled Madame Dumont who had her own gaming tables where were played faro, keno, monte and poker. Her place was open day and night on Broad Street. Sometimes gamblers wagered at her tables ten thousand dollars in dust.

In this first theatre of Nevada City frequently was seated a distinguished group of men: Stephen J. Field, first assemblyman and later of the United States Supreme Court; Aaron A. Sargent, publisher of the Nevada City *Journal* and later United States Senator; Supreme Judge Niles Searls, T. B. McFarland and Lorenzo Sawyer. The last named was afterward United States Circuit Judge. In those days "Bill" Stewart was everywhere. He and Hearst became great friends. Stewart went to the Senate from Nevada and was Hearst's attorney in Nevada mining litigation. Senator William M. Stewart paid a beautiful tribute to Senator George Hearst as a final act of respect for his friend after his death in Washington.

Shortly after Hearst arrived in Nevada City, a fire burned most of the buildings. They were immediately rebuilt, and Nevada City became a real city with a charter, a post office, a private school and a Methodist Church on the hill with eight or ten women in the congregation. These women insured a large attendance of men. Hamlet Davis, Hearst's partner in the store and theatre, was elected the first mayor. Nevada City became the county seat in May 1851, with a judge, a sheriff and a "regular law outfit."

Hearst now became The-Man-That-Earth-Talked-To. His instinct for mineralogy, together with his boyhood experience while mining for lead in Missouri, combined to aid him when he located a ledge on the dividing line between Nevada City and Grass Valley. This ledge has ever since been known as Merrimac Hill. Hearst gave it that name, with the variation in spelling, in memory of the river in which he learned to swim as a boy, the stream that so satisfied his sense of beauty and gave him pleasure in childhood sports. When he found Merrimac ledge he had that old "lucky" feeling. Immediately the ledge yielded rich gold specimens near the surface, as do all the good Mother Lode mines; "picture gold," the miners called it. Hearst perfected the legal title to the ledge, formed a company, and began work on his first quartz mine. Now he knew he would be a millionaire.

# THE FOURTEENTH CHAPTER

GEORGE HEARST always worked quietly, but with great certainty and enthusiasm. He understood workmen. They liked him and had faith in him. When he took possession of the Merrimac Hill Mine, he directed his men skillfully, but he toiled and sweated with them as he had toiled and sweated with his men in the fields of Missouri. He always knew how to do a thing a trifle better and a trifle more swiftly than any of his employees. One day Hearst and his men drove the shaft downward nineteen feet. In those days of quartz mining it was an achievement not approached for a long time. Nevada City realized that another great miner had arrived from Missouri.

Hearst, himself, declared that the Missouri school of practical mining was one of the best to graduate from. Missouri mining regulations controlled the Mother Lode. Missourians acquired their mining laws from the French, the first miners of their state. Knowledge of fair size claims, the way to hold them, the regulations respecting them, Hearst said was brought to California by Missourians.

After the shaft on the Merrimac had been sunk thirty feet, water was struck. It was generally thought that ledges could not be worked profitably below water. The correct theory of quartz-bearing lodes was yet to be worked out. After yielding richly, the Merrimac Ledge was temporarily abandoned at a depth of thirty feet, but to be developed later.

Meanwhile, Hearst located another mine on Gold Flat, near Nevada City, not far from Merrimac Hill. This mine was called the Potosi — not, as has been thought, after the famous Bolivian mines, but after a mine Hearst knew well in Washington County, Missouri. He was associated in this mine with Rufus Shoemaker, a man who later became prominent in Nevada City as County Clerk and editor of the Grass Valley *National.*

Hearst made his first "clean-up" with the Merrimac and the Potosi. The winter of 1851 and 1852 was severe throughout the northern mines. Torrents of rain and blinding snow drove the miners to the shelter of their cabins. Roads became impassable. Provisions in the stores were running low. Food cost as much as it had on the Overland Trail. A dollar a pound was charged for everything, except beef, which was fifty cents. Work was impossible in the mines. Never had Hearst thought he could rest, unless he was ill. For the first time he determined to take a vacation and spend the winter in Sacramento, the future capital. He had the thrill of going on a tour of the world. He was glad to live in the town, to sleep in a bed once more, to get something better than camp fare, and have a few months of rest and recreation.

But Hearst could not rest, even for a few months. In Missouri, and in Nevada City, he had dabbled in merchandising. In Sacramento he invested his earnings in a general merchandising business. Under the firm name of "Hearst & Company, Wholesale Merchants" he opened a store at 92 K Street, and made his home on the premises. It is a coincidence that four future United States Senators should have lived in Sacramento at this time. Leland Stanford had a store at 58 K Street, only a few doors from Hearst. Newton Booth, uncle of the unborn famous novelist, Booth Tarkington, was the senior member of Booth and Company, wholesale merchants in the same block. Near the building of Leland Stanford, Cornelius Cole was practicing law. Milton S. Latham was a lawyer in the Tehama Block.

George Hearst was never intended to be a merchant. He couldn't get excited over "one bit" or "two bits" or "four bits." His storekeeping on the Old Springfield Road in Missouri had not been a success. His was too broad and expansive a spirit to refuse credit. Petty details harassed him. Only big projects interested Hearst. His third attempt at storekeeping was his last. It was a failure, and he was free from the tyranny of trade. He never liked cities, and herds of people. He was glad to leave Sacramento, which in March 1852, had a disastrous flood. He regretted the gold dust from the Merrimac and the Potosi sunk in Sacramento merchandising, but he had the compensation of experience. He knew that there was more gold waiting for him in the mountains. Never again would he try to be a merchant. After all he was not a Yankee. He was a Missourian and South Carolinian. When the rainy season was over he gladly went back to the mines.

Hearst returned to Nevada City and Grass Valley and worked the Merrimac Mine superficially in order to retain it under the quartz laws of the county. He knew it was a good mine, but it would cost more money to develop than he at that time could command. Later he sold his interest to Joseph Woodworth, Thomas Findley, Henry Scaden, A. E. Head and George D. Roberts. Roberts became an important figure in California mining. At one time he owned the great Empire Mine. He was first to use quicksilver on the tables of a quartz mill. The discovery was soon adopted everywhere. The new owners of the Merrimac developed the property, put in a ten stamp mill, tunneled the ground for a distance of eight hundred feet, and made a large sum.

The Potosi also proved to be an important mining property. Later Hearst sold it, and it netted large returns to the owner.

During Hearst's absence in Sacramento, Nevada City had become a big town with six stores, two jewelry shops, two bakeries, five hotels. It was a pleasant place in which to live. Saturday and Sunday nights were lively. Two or three thousand red-shirted miners, wearing duck overalls, filled the streets and gambling houses. No one "dressed up" except gamblers or lawyers. Hearst lived in Nevada City for the next five years. He was associated with Roberts and his cousins, the Clarks. They devoted themselves to prospecting, locating, developing and selling mines in the rich country of Deer and Wolf Creeks. They all made comfortable fortunes, but in the year 1857 Hearst found their first big mine. With his usual modesty he described it in this way: "We got a good mine in Nevada County, and put up a mill and made some money out of it." This was the LeCompton. In order to reach this mine he traveled three miles from Nevada City up the steep, narrow Deer Creek trail. Here, tucked away at the base of a mountan, is the mine that made his first fortune. This section became known as the LeCompton District.

The name LeCompton came from the LeCompton party in California, the party of Gwin and Terry, but it had a Missourian association. The LeCompton party took its name from Senator Samuel Dexter LeCompte, a popular Missourian.

Though Hearst did not go home, his thoughts were seldom far from Franklin County and his mother. He had now been in California seven years, and he promised himself that the next year, and then the next, he would go to Missouri to see his mother. Something always detained him in California. There was ever one more achievement to complete before he went home. Elizabeth Hearst always dreamed that George would come in the spring, or in the autumn. George did not go, but he followed the life of the state.

After Hearst acquired the LeCompton Mine, news of the Washoe Country strike was wafted over the mountains as a rumor. But then, his Scotch caution said, there were always new excitements in mining camps. He had learned to discount them all. John Stone and W. P. Morrison, of Nevada City, went to the Washoe Country, discovered a ledge, and Morrison returned with specimens for J. J. Ott to assay. The assaying was done in secret. It showed fifteen hundred and ninety-five dollars gold and thirty-one hundred and ninety-six dollars silver to the ton. These startling assays were whispered. They had all the pungency of truth. Hearst wondered if he should go to Nevada.

Finally a mule load of "heavy black stuff" was brought to Melville Atwood, an assayer in Nevada City. Atwood was a friend of Hearst's. Atwood assayed it, told him in secret that the ore was almost pure silver, with a heavy percentage of gold. Atwood was so amazed that he doubted both his chemistry and his calculations. The ore was worth three thousand dollars a ton, and Washoe miners were throwing it away! Hearst consulted his friend, A. E. Head. Atwood, the mining expert decided that the heavy black ore was too incredibly rich to be possible. This decision caused Hearst and Head to determine to go to Washoe to see the discovery ground.

Washoe was a hundred miles over the mountains. There were threats of Indian warfare, but Hearst, A. E. Head, Melville Atwood, and Judge Walsh, set out on muleback to make the journey. They thought it would take four or five days.

Hearst had no enthusiasm for the trip, even though they all declared they were certain to be rich. He could not forget the Nevada, which he had toiled through years before. He recalled the white, blinding sand and the blistering heat that choked him and drained his energy, the spare soil, the dusty sagebrush, the terrible thirst, the sun that baked him alive, set fire to his brain, and laid him low with fever. Must he sweat and crawl back over that terrible way?

Even after they had set out on the steep climb Hearst rode along thinking. He fell behind his companions. He got off his mule, sat on a log, and let the dust run through his fingers. He remained there twenty minutes or more playing with that dust. Was that "heavy black stuff" a hoax? In Nevada City the future was secure, but beyond in the barren desert mountains, what was certain but an ever growing possiblity of Indian warfare? Wasn't it all a wild goose chase?

Suddenly that "lucky" feeling again came to Hearst. The earth, the "heavy black stuff" of the ledges of Nevada seemed to speak to and summon him. He mounted and went on a gallop to Nevada and to fortune.

## THE FIFTEENTH CHAPTER

IN 1859 unborn Nevada was still western Utah. During that year Sun Peak, in western Utah, later called Mount Davidson in honor of the San Francisco agent of the Rothschild family, became the center of the new frenzied mining fever. Sun Peak was a tawny, treeless, glaring summit rising in brazen sunlight to an elevation of seven thousand, eight hundred and twenty feet. It was thirty miles from Genoa, a Mormon settlement, and one hundred miles from Sacramento. When George Hearst went over the Sierra Nevada down to Carson, passed Genoa, and toiled that blistering way upward and saw Sun Peak, he did not realize that he was looking at a mountain which would later change the history of the United States. After the Civil War the gold and silver yield of this vast deposit enabled the United States to resume specie payment.

Hearst and his friends, mounted on pack mules with blankets, picks, shovels, hammers and frying pans, arrived at Sun Peak, pioneers of the great backward rush from California. Hearst saw a tent where people were working. He did not know it, but he was looking at the Comstock, the beginning of a new state. At this time there were about a thousand people in western Utah. The region was known by the Indian name, Wasseau. The Mormons called it Wassaw, afterward Washoe.

Pagans would say that George Hearst had arrived as usual at the lucky moment. Christians would say that he was providentially guided. Before George Hearst came Sun Peak had a dark history. Tragedy followed those daring to wrest from its barren flanks the rich mineral deposits.

In 1849 two brothers, E. Allen Grosch and Hosea B. Grosch of Reading, Pennsylvania, trained mineralogists, sons of a Universalist preacher, were mining in El Lorado County, California. In 1851 they prospected the placers of what came to be known as Gold Canyon. In the gold of this canyon they found a great mass of black rock. They wrote down that they thought it contained silver.

In 1853 the Grosch brothers looked for gold in Carson, Lake and Washoe Valleys. In 1857 they built themselves a stone cabin in American Flat Ravine. They were waiting to be joined by a partner named Brown, who kept the mail station at Gravelly Ford on the Humboldt River. Brown had some capital that he had promised to put into the development of their claim. He never arrived. He was murdered.

About this time Hosea Grosch stuck a pick into his foot. Blood poisoning resulted, and he died September 2, 1857. In the middle of November Allen Grosch set out for California to raise money for a mining company. He was caught in a terrible snowstorm, and was compelled to kill and eat his pack mule. He abandoned his baggage and specimens, and wandered about in the snow for eleven days. Finally he reached the camp of a Mexican miner, his legs frozen above the knees. He died December 19, 1857.

Allen Grosch left his mine in charge of William Thomas Page Comstock. He was called "Old Pancake" Comstock because he would never take the time to make bread. Even as he stirred his pancake batter it was said that he kept one eye on distant Sun Peak and talked of the gold and silver hidden under its rocky crest. From childhood "Old Pancake" had trapped and hunted. He had fought in the Black Hawk, Patriot and Mexican Wars. He was generally thought to be half mad. After Allen Grosch's death all evidence of the Grosch ownership disappeared. "Old Pancake" Comstock assumed charge. Until 1858 he stood guard in Gold Canyon over the Grosch claim.

Prospecting went on. In 1857 a number of men from Gold Canyon had found a new field about a mile below the ground now occupied by Virginia City. Among these prospectors was James Fennimore, alias Finney, a drunken Virginian, called by the miners "Old Virginia." In company with Fennimore were Peter O'Riley, Patrick McLaughlin, Joseph Kirby and Nicholas Ambrose. These men prospected Gold Canyon in 1859, accompanied by "Old Pancake" Comstock.

In January 1859, Comstock, Fennimore, Bishop and others staked off their claims, and called the section Gold Hill. They were somewhat annoyed because the quartz worked by them was almost black. They knew there was gold, but in the rocker along with the gold was a quantity of "heavy black stuff." They were bothered because it clogged the rocker and interfered with washing gold dust. They threw it away. There is a legend that a dark, heavy-lidded, wily Mexican, named Maldonado, who had mined in Mexico before coming to California, inspected it and remarked that it looked like silver sulfide.

For about a week the miners worked the rich, decomposed ore. They thought it would soon be exhausted, but on the eleventh of June they came to a solid ledge four feet wide. A man named Penrod declared it to be a quartz vein. The others objected to locating it as quartz. Comstock finally agreed with Penrod that it was quartz. They gave notice of their claims, which included fifteen hundred feet on the ledge, three hundred feet for each man, and three hundred additional for the discoverer, according to the mining laws of California.

Comstock talked loudly about his lode. He called it the Comstock Lode. Many located claims upon it. The ore was sent to Nevada City to be assayed. Penrod, Comstock and Company christened their mine the Ophir. Very soon the Mexican, Gabriel Maldonado, with his farseeing, deep eyes bought Penrod's share for three thousand dollars. The Ophir was the first claim recorded on the Comstock Lode.

Early in June, being short of water, the owners excavated a small reservoir a short distance above their claim. This water to be collected for rocker use was from a rivulet. Comstock told his partners that the spring they wished to use was owned by Penrod, Fennimore (Old Virginia) and himself. He also declared that the ground on which their discovery was made belonged to Fennimore, Joseph Kirby, James White and William Hart. He proposed to buy off these persons and to organize a firm consisting of Penrod, McLaughlin and himself. By this coup Comstock controlled both water and the claim. Penrod paid three of the owners fifty dollars each for their water rights. Comstock purchased Fennimore's interest in the spring for an old, blind horse. Joseph D. Winters, seeing that the rocker continued to wash out rich specimens, found the missing share owner and bought his right without informing him of its value. Winters was admitted as a partner.

George Hearst arrived at the Ophir before its value was realized. People could not believe that this queer "black stuff" was silver; it looked too much like lead. Most people thought it was of no account. Hearst had worked in lead mines. He recognized that there was a great deal of lead in the ore because it had not been refined. Again the earth seemed to speak to him. He realized that the ore was very valuable. He held to his belief in spite of the fact that the doubters said that some swindlers had brought this queer "black stuff" up from Mexico and planted it on Sun Peak in order to cheat unsuspecting miners. Hearst inspected the quartz carefully, and contracted to buy from McLaughlin a sixth interest in the Ophir. He had no ready money to pay with, and so he got on his mule and rode back to Nevada City. With him were Head and Atwood, also partners in the Ophir. All three had saddlebags filled with the queer "black stuff."

In Nevada City Hearst sold his interest in his "little mine," the LeCompton, to McLane and Givens, who in turn disposed of it to J. J. Ott, the assayer. Hearst borrowed a thousand dollars from a hotel keeper in Nevada City. Then he took leave of the place where he had made his first comfortable fortune. Their hearts beating with hopes of new achievement, the three men mounted mules and turned toward Sun Peak. Hearst later recalled that on the return journey to the Ophir they found a man on the bank of the Truckee riddled with lead. They paused and nursed him, and then went on their way. Within a few months not one of the original owners of the Ophir had any share in it, nor had the new company as yet any conception of the magnitude of its riches. They did not dream that a giant lode pierced the mountain from side to side.

A town sprang up about the Ophir mine named Ophir. Comstock afterward called it Silver City, but by a roistering whim of Fennimore's it became Virginia Town after Old Virginia himself. It is said that one night Old Virginia, with some of his friends, got drunk. He fell down and broke his whiskey bottle. When Old Virginia got up he said solemnly he had baptized in whiskey the ground Virginia City. A month later, when the town had eight stone houses, it was proposed to christen it Winnemucca after the Pah-Ute chieftain of that name. The idea was unpopular, and Virginia City was finally adopted.

Poor Old Virginia was killed at Dayton, Nevada, in July 1861, by being thrown from his horse while intoxicated. "Old Pancake" Comstock married the eloping plural wife of a Mormon. When she ran away from him, Comstock committed suicide in Montana.

Soon white, glaring, western Utah became a roaring mining camp, with Virginia City, its metropolis, proudly commanding a mountain amphitheatre. The new city had no hotel, and only one restaurant where half a dozen persons at a time were supplied with poor meals at seventy-five cents. Travelers found lodgings by spreading their blankets on the east side of Sun Peak. So many people hurried to the new diggings that during the summers of 1859 and 1860 many lived in excavations in the earth. By this time George Hearst was called "lucky." Wherever he went there was good fortune. Half of Nevada City followed him and his partners into the Washoe country. Hearst had two arastras made ready for the Ophir. These arastras were mills for quartz, propelled by horses or mules. The new owners of the Ophir put every penny they could raise into getting ore out of the mine. Some questioned the soundness of the venture. It was hard to believe that the black ore was incredibly rich in gold and silver. Hearst had confidence in Atwood's assays. Surely there was gold, and an even greater abundance of silver. How to extract the silver—that was the problem. Hearst knew it could be done.

Forty-five tons were quickly taken out of the Ophir. Several heavy samples were made ready to be transported on muleback. George Hearst and his associates mounted mules and conveyed the ore. This was in the bitter winter of 1859.

Three miles out of Nevada City the snow was twelve to eighteen feet deep. Lower down in the valley rain beat down in driving floods. California had not had such a winter since 1849. The heavy-laden mules plodded on over the trails. Hearst had endured all the most trying forms of travel. In comparison with crossing the plains, staggering forward in spite of cholera and fever, this was a pleasant jaunt. Besides, he thrilled at the thought that he was going to San Francisco. He had never seen a large city. What adventure! Perhaps he was entering San Francisco with a vast fortune! If the ore was as rich as Atwood's assays showed, soon he would go back to Missouri to see his mother. Nearly ten years had passed since he took leave of her at the ford of the Gasconade.

He felt that he would be with her again. Hearst, Head and Atwood left the mules at Sacramento and boarded the river steamer with their ore for San Francisco.

It was a strange, helter-skelter, ill-paved, sprawling city, with Powell Street at the upper end of the town, and Montgomery Street the important thoroughfare. George Hearst was forty, tall, erect, with fine, wide-open eyes, long beard and a broad-brimmed hat. It was his first appearance on Montgomery Street, the street where he was to be so great a power. He was a stranger from Missouri, Hangtown, Nevada City, Virginia City, but he strode down the street like a ruler who had come into his kingdom. Many turned and gazed after him, as people turned and gazed after him until the day of his death. He looked like the plains, like the mountains, like California, like Utah, like Nevada, like Dakota, like Montana, like the great Far West where by force of his strength and intelligence and genius he was to reign.

The Comstock ore brought by Hearst to San Francisco would change history, but he tramped the streets of the Golden Gate city vainly seeking to find some one to handle it. Smelter managers looked at the heavy "black stuff" and sniffed. They had never seen anything like it. The firm of Donald Davidson and Company, San Francisco agents for the Rothschilds, superciliously offered to ship the strange stuff to England, naming a heavy price. George Hearst declined their proposal. Within five years the Rothschilds were clamoring to invest in the Comstock.

After a long search Hearst discovered a German chemist who offered to build a furnace and smelt the ore for four hundred and fifty dollars a ton. His offer was accepted. The furnace was erected. Pack mules brought in sacks on their sturdy backs, the entire forty-five tons from Virginia City. The freight cost was twenty-four thousand dollars.

The smelting began. At last the smelted ore of the Ophir was ready. Hearst, Head and Atwood anxiously took the precious "black stuff" to the mint. Days of nervous waiting passed. Were they credulous fools, or were they to be millionaires?

Finally C. H. Hemstead, the Superintendent of the Mint, sent this message: "Boys, come up tonight and I will give you some money." The ore had yielded twenty-two hundred dollars a ton. There were eighty thousand glittering, clinking, wonderful Sun Peak dollars, money made out of the queer "black stuff" shoveled out of the earth. The belly of the great barren Sun Peak in the Washoe country was bursting with more.

Hearst and his friends filled their pockets full, hurried down town, went up and down Montgomery Street, to find out if the money would pass for whiskey. It did.

This was March 1860. It was another Forty-Nine. The Washoe excitement began. From one end of the Pacific Coast to another the shout was set up, "Silver in Washoe!" Ledges ten thousand feet deep! A solid mass of silver! Nevada City hurried over the mountains. Diamond Springs moved to the Comstock. So did Hangtown. So did Sacramento. So did San Francisco. So did John W. Mackay and James G. Fair, young miners.

By April 1860, George Hearst was back at the Ophir. He had a hard trip through the snow. The Ophir Mining Company had already been formed, with eleven shareholders. They employed ten laborers, taking out a ton of sulphurets and about eight tons of quartz. Some of the pieces of sulphurets brought ten thousand dollars a ton.

The general richness of the vein varied from fifteen hundred to ten thousand dollars a ton, the average being three thousand. The vein ran five portions of silver to one of gold.

In 1860 the Ophir Company installed steam hoisting and pumping equipment, driven by a fifteen horsepower donkey engine. It was worked through an inclined shaft, following the dip of a vein, up which the ore was hoisted. Before the year was over a depth of one hundred and eighty feet was reached. The post and cap supports, common in California mines where used. The ore body was found to be of the unprecedented breadth of forty-five feet. Timbers of sufficient length and strength to prevent the sinking of the roof of the mine over so wide a space could not be obtained, even if they had the required durability to make them safe.

This serious difficulty was overcome by a German mining engineer, Philip Deidesheimer. He framed timbers together in square sets, forming cribs four by six feet in size, which could be piled upon one another to any height and which would resist lateral as well as downward pressure. These cribs were filled with waste rock, and could be made enduring pillars, reaching the length of the deepest mine. These Deidesheimer cribs were precisely what the Comstock Lode needed for its complete development.

The Ophir was the center of Virginia City. Hearst and his associates felt that Sun Peak was the peak of the world. And it was.

Then came rumbling rumors that Pah-Utes were on the warpath. The Indians were starving. During the cold winter of 1859 and 1860 the white men's cattle had eaten all the grass. There was no seed for bread. The white men had cut down the Indians' pine nut trees, which were their orchards. The Indians were dying and cold. Some white men gave the Indians food, built them large fires. But the Pah-Utes preferred to freeze. They would not eat the food of the hated white man. They said it had been poisoned. Chief Winnemucca and nearly all the Utah chiefs demanded war.

Then Peter Lassen, for whom Lassen Peak was named, was killed by the Bannocks. The whites raged.

Mogoannoga, chief of the Humboldt Meadows men, formerly known as Captain Soo, opened the war. He attacked Williams' Station, on the Overland road. The war was on. California was appealed to, and sent aid.

Major William M. Ormsby was in charge of the whites. He was killed in the battle of Pyramid Lake. The Indians shot sixty-five out of a hundred white men in two fights.

Women and children of Virginia City were placed in an unfinished stone house for protection. Many miners fled to California. The mines were shut down.

The war became bloodier. Men, women and children, immigrants, were killed by the Indians eight miles east of Gravelly Ford, and their bodies were cast into the Humboldt. White men kidnapped the Indian women. Indians killed the cattle of the white men. The order was given: "Shoot all male Indians. Take no prisoners. We'll run the Indians out of the country."

Provisions soared to unheard-of prices. It was impossible to get workmen. In the midst of this Indian warfare Hearst received a letter from his mother in Missouri. His sister, Patsy, was dead. His mother was gravely ill. She called her son to her side.

Hearst had largely worked for his mother. He was, inspired by the desire to make her happy. The fact that she could be on earth only a short time made his possessions seem without value. What was the Comstock Lode when a dying mother called?

Hearst sold a part of his interest in the Ophir for sixteen thousand dollars. In June of 1860 he hurried to San Francisco and took the Panama steamer for home.

# THE SIXTEENTH CHAPTER

In May 1850, Elizabeth Collins Hearst blessed her son and kissed him goodbye at the ford of the Gasconade River. He set out with glamorous hopes, and ten years later he brought back to the old Missouri homestead substantial achievement. He stepped across his mother's threshold and was folded in her arms. How pale, fair, beautiful and faraway she looked with death shadowed on her brow.

But he did not call it death. Now his mother would not die. She could not die. He would bring back her strength. Always he had tried to shelter her and protect her and save her from a troubled life. Ten years had passed. It seemed that he had never been away. They had always been together. They always would be together. He would sell his mine. He would never go back to California and Utah. If he did go, he would take his mother with him. Elizabeth Hearst forgot that she was mortally stricken. Her son gave her new life. Yes, when she felt stronger she would go to California with him.

This mother and son were much alike. They responded to the same moods and music of life. They could not cease talking. All over again they lived the past ten years, the immigrant trail, buffaloes, Indians, flooded rivers, mountain summits, glaring deserts. Then Hangtown, Nevada City, Sacramento, San Francisco, towns of gold; Carson, Washoe, Virginia City, towns of silver. The cholera, the fever, the struggle, the toil, the hunger, the backaches, the disappointments, the despair—these Hearst scarcely touched upon. He described a fairyland of glittering rainbows where people trod on gold and silver. From a five franc piece to the great Ophir mine! Wonderful!

But his mother always knew that this son would end in precisely this way. Had he not penned the sheep in the fold? Had he not always been her man-child? She and he talked of Father and Patsy and Philip, and of the old days before the log cabin disappeared, of spinning and weaving, of plucking geese to make feather beds, of beating out flax before the fire. They forgot everything but those beautiful old days when hunger made food delicious and the winter's cold made the cabin beautiful. And as they talked the old days of poverty seemed more wonderful than California and the Comstock.

For miles the neighbors came to welcome George Hearst, to see the nuggets brought by him, to touch them, and touching them to make the vow that they would go to California. The old Negro slaves came to shake Marse George by the hand. There was talk of war and of emancipation of slaves. George Hearst bought emancipation for his old slaves, and built them comfortable cabins.

During the winter of 1861 there often came to the

bedside of Elizabeth Hearst her namesake, Puss, now grown to be Miss Phoebe Elizabeth Apperson, seventeen, and teaching school in St. James, Missouri. George Hearst had not seen her since she was seven, when she was a lovely, graceful child. Ten years had made her a lovely, graceful woman. When she came into his mother's house she looked somewhat like a face of the Blessed Virgin that he had seen in a shrine in a French mine when he was a boy.

Now Phoebe Elizabeth Apperson was mystical, different from the women he had seen in the past ten years; determined, rugged women of the prairie schooners; women of the fandango houses; women who could use a rocker like a man. Phoebe Elizabeth Apperson was a vision. She had grace and charm and touches of humor like his own. Though she had been brought up in the log-cabin country she could play the piano. She stammered French. She was eager to learn. She used to hold a book in her left hand and churn with her right. She was sure of herself. She was not afraid of him. He was almost a kinsman, her cousin's cousin. She wished to hear about George Hearst's experiences. Had he really been obliged to flee from Indians? How many times did he barely escape death? What was the Pacific Ocean like? And San Francisco? And New York? And the Atlantic? What a traveled man he was! But, she said to herself, best of all, how tall he was! She herself was short. She had made up her mind that she would never marry any but a tall man.

That winter Phoebe Apperson came often. Sometimes she drove, but usually she rode. And George Hearst often rode back to St. James by her side. He was always a silent man, and she was never a chatterbox. They used to ride long distances without speaking. They understood each other. Elizabeth Collins Hearst knew they understood each other. She was happy. She wished to see her namesake the wife of her son before she died.

Randolph Walker Apperson of Virginia, and his wife, Drucilla Whitmire Apperson of South Carolina, had quite a different point of view. They considered George Hearst almost middle-aged. Phoebe was barely eighteen. Youth should marry youth. Besides, George would return to faraway California and that terrible Mormon country, Utah, where Brigham Young lived with goodness knew how many wives. Phoebe should never live in such wild places. She should marry someone from Franklin County, or at the farthest, St. Louis. They were a trifle cool to George Hearst when he came to call. What did he mean by coming to see Phoebe? Phoebe knew. The Clarks knew. Some of them had been to California with George Hearst and returned well-to-do. They thought that Phoebe would be lucky to marry George. They told the Appersons. The Appersons became emphatic. Phoebe should not marry George Hearst. Both Phoebe Apperson and George Hearst were definite, decisive people. They continued to ride together. It was the first time in his whole life that George Hearst ever played. This playtime lasted six months. George hoped that the Appersons would soften their objections. He didn't speak of marriage.

As winter wore on, George Hearst saw that his mother would go with the coming of spring. Love could not conquer death. It was long years since he had prayed, but even prayers silent and intense could not stay death. One day Elizabeth Collins Hearst looked at her son with eyes opened wide, as if she saw through all space and all time. "George, I will meet you in heaven," she said. She never spoke again.

After George Hearst left his mother in the Dry Branch Cemetery with his father, brother and sister, he knew that nothing remained for him in Missouri but Phoebe Apperson. She was still called Puss, as always she had been in her childhood, but he liked to say Phoebe Elizabeth because Elizabeth recalled his mother. A few days after the funeral he told Phoebe that he was going to California and he wished to take her with him as his wife. She said yes. The Appersons said no. She said yes again. More firmly the Appersons said no. For the last time she said yes, and for the last time most emphatically the Appersons said no.

George Hearst would not accept no. Phoebe Elizabeth Apperson would not accept no. She said she was going to California with George Hearst.

The marriage was performed on June 15, 1862, at Steelville, Missouri. Phoebe Apperson thought she was going to live in the mines and dress like a miner's wife. Perhaps she would be living in a tent or a cabin. With some of her money earned teaching school she bought herself material for a brown merina dress to make on the way to California.

George Hearst looked at the plain, brown merino dress and inwardly smiled. He had been too modest to tell her about the Ophir with ore at ten thousand dollars a ton. His bride did not know. That should be her surprise. In September 1862, George Hearst and his bride left for New York City to sail for California by way of the Isthmus of Panama.

# THE SEVENTEENTH CHAPTER

GEORGE HEARST enjoyed showing his eager young bride their country. She allowed nothing to escape her observant gray-blue eyes. There was Chicago, so booming and bustling that it made St. Louis seem like the lazy old French Southern town that it was. Then came New York, with Fifth Avenue, its brownstone fronts, handsome hotels, liveried servants, beautiful, smart women and the glitter of the great metropolis.

The steamer sailing from New York to Panama was not a huge European liner. It was a small vessel ill-equipped for the rough, wild Atlantic. Phoebe Apperson Hearst, the girl-bride, went aboard joyously. She walked on tiptoe. Never before had she seen the ocean. How exhilarating it smelled. At last, she was going to see the world.

The steamer sailed, and the young wife fell ill. The Captain said he had never seen anyone so desperately ill of seasickness. George Hearst did not know what to do for his sick, young bride.

On the steamer were Mr. and Mrs. David Peck and

their two children who were going to San Francisco to live. Mrs. Peck was a motherly, gentle woman. She offered her services in nursing Mrs. Hearst and enabled her to bear the journey. Hearst was most appreciative. He was fond of children, and he took a fancy to the Peck children. One of them was Orrin Peck, who later became a celebrated portrait painter, and one of William Randolph Hearst's closest friends. The other Peck child was Helen, who in after years was Mrs. Frederick Sanborn, and deeply beloved in San Francisco. The two families always cherished tenderly their friendship born on the buffeting stormy Atlantic.

By the time the ship finally docked Phoebe once more entered into the joy of living. Gladly she boarded the little train at Aspinwall that crossed to Panama. This was before the days of inoculation against fever. Hundreds of travelers and gold-seekers had been buried on that Isthmus, but this did not deter those young, enthusiastic, lighthearted people. To these youngsters even the miasma in the air, the insects with the deadly sting, the white mist from the black, sodden earth poisoning wayfarers, was just one jolly experience. It was all a part of going to the land of dreams and dreamers, California. Gorgeous green and red parrots malignantly screeched warning from the trees, but Phoebe Hearst enjoyed it all, even the monkeys, swinging from tree to tree, and the strange serpents. She thought the moist tropical jungle beautiful. She was glad she came to see this new strange land. She could hardly believe that she was she, so different was this Panama world from Franklin County, Missouri. And her big husband shared in her joy.

The Pacific was much calmer than the Atlantic. The

seasickness abated, and now Phoebe Hearst could settle down to finish that brown merino dress. She must get it ready to wear in the mining camps of California and Nevada. She was a dexterous needlewoman, and she intended to make all her own dresses. She had never paid so much attention to making anything as she did to this brown merino dress. She was sewing not only for herself, but for her husband's approval. She sewed while the ship crawled up the west coast and she looked out on distant volcanoes. She sewed while they steamed northward over silent, tropic seas filled with huge torpid turtles. At last, the dress, with its puffs and ruffles, was finished. She showed it to George Hearst. He told her it was great.

Phoebe Hearst never forgot the wonderful day when, through the mist, she saw the California coast. Nor did she ever forget her entrance through the Golden Gate, nor looking out for the first time on the city of countless hills. George Hearst pointed them out to her, told her how he had tramped over those hills trying to find a smelter for his ore. There were Rincon Hill, Telegraph Hill, Twin Peaks and Russian Hill. Phoebe Apperson Hearst was born among hills. She was not afraid of them. She looked at Russian Hill, and with an instinctive sense of beauty said: "Russian Hill is where I'd like to live." It was prophetic. Eventually she did live on a lower portion of Russian Hill.

In those days before the transcontinental railroad trains, the arrival of the Panama steamer was a great event in San Francisco. When the ship came in, waiting San Francisco rushed aboard. The steamer docked at the rickety, little wooden wharf, and Phoebe Hearst saw San Francisco, which was always to be her home. There were velvet-footed Chinese with long queues, wearing bright mandarin coats. There were Indians in blankets, and Mexicans with sombreros. There were American dandies, in silk hats and broadcloth, and bearded miners. Soft-voiced Southern women, and high-nosed executive New England women, tripped on board to welcome friends. These Southern ladies and these New England ladies looked at each other frigidly. It was the time of the Civil War, and in San Francisco there was bitter feeling between the sympathizers of North and South.

In 1862 San Francisco had a population of eighty thousand. Montgomery Street was the important business thoroughfare. Here strolled Emperor Norton with "Bummer" and "Lazarus," his licensed pet dogs. Between Montgomery and Kearny Streets on Sacramento, Clay and Washington, were fashionable shops for women. Market Street was scarcely inhabited. St. Patrick's Church, and the Roman Catholic Orphan Asylum, stood on the site of the future Palace Hotel. St. Ignatius Church was in St. Anne's Valley, a depression in the sand dunes where the Emporium now stands. A single track steam railroad ran from Second Street to distant Mission Dolores. Yerba Buena Cemetery, a gore of sixteen acres bounded by Market, Larkin and McAllister Streets, recently had been closed, a park being in contemplation. Omnibuses ran from the Plaza (Portsmouth Square) to Lone Mountain, Mission Dolores, the Presidio and Fort Point. A cross-town line ran between North Beach and South Park, the latter fast becoming a fashionable residence quarter. The handsomest dwellings were on Rincon Hill. Nob Hill had not yet been named by Denis Kearney.

There was a Seal Rock House, but no Cliff House. Amusements were inexpensive. Family parties spent

Sundays at The Willows, in the block bounded by Valencia and Mission, Eighteenth and Nineteenth (then called Falcon and Eagle) Streets; or at Russ Gardens where Columbia Park is now. The boisterous lovers of sport spent Sundays at the Mission, in cock-fighting, racing and bull-baiting. The best theatres were the Metropolitan on Montgomery between Washington and Jackson Streets, the American at the southeast corner of Sansome and Halleck, and Maguire's Opera House on Washington near Montgomery. There were five principal dailies: *Alta California, Call* and *Herald* (morning), and *Bulletin and Journal* (evening). Henry George was an obscure writer. Francis Bret Harte was a clerk in the office of United States Surveyor-General Edward F. Beale. Charles Warren Stoddard was clerking for Beach, the bookseller, on Montgomery Street. John C. Frémont, the Pathfinder, had a home at Black Point.

H. F. Teschemacher was Mayor. Leland Stanford, Hearst's old Sacramento acquaintance, was War Governor. Milton S. Latham and James A. McDougall were United States Senators.

To this San Francisco George Hearst brought his bride. He escorted his wife to a carriage, commonly called a "hack." They drove to the Lick House, the finest hotel on the Pacific Coast. The young bride was dazzled by the mirrors, the velvet, the plush, the shining brass and the carved furniture of the ladies' parlor, such as she had never seen except in her flight through New York. She was almost breathless with surprise when her husband told her that they were to live at the Lick House. How could they afford it?

George Hearst smiled and answered that he would try. Young Mrs. Hearst wished to wear her brown merino

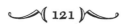

dress, but George Hearst told her that he would like to buy her a real gown. Again he ordered a hack. Such extravagance frightened the young wife. They drove to The White House, where her measurements were taken. Grandly but, young Mrs. Hearst thought, recklessly, George ordered made for her a black silk dress. The bride said she had never seen anything so wonderful as this heavy black silk, trimmed with white lace. No sooner had young Mrs. Hearst worn her black silk dress to the theatre than another great parcel was delivered to the bride—a pearl-gray silk dress. This, too, came from The White House. It was followed by a green silk. Then came a blue satin gown, shoes, hats, packages of gloves, a fan, costly trinkets and baubles, until finally Phoebe Apperson Hearst, in alarm, took counsel with her oldest friend in California, Mrs. David Peck.

What should she do? Why did her husband send these costly dresses? What was the matter with him? Surely he would go bankrupt. Young Mrs. Hearst wished to wear her brown merino dress. It was sensible and economical. She had tried to keep George from buying presents for her, but the more she protested, the more he bought.

The bride found out the awful truth when Mrs. Peck answered: "Don't worry, dear, your husband is part owner in one of the richest mines of the West."

# THE EIGHTEENTH CHAPTER

GEORGE HEARST was fortunate, even in his wife. She had beauty, intelligence and a generous grace that made him many friends. When she discovered that she had no need to economize, she began seeking out the best there was in art and music in San Francisco. Just as always in Franklin County she sought whatever culture the community offered, so in San Francisco she hungrily studied French, history, politics, art, literature, architecture, the drama, the opera. Young as she was, living in a gay city, with youth, beauty, fortune, she had no share in frivolity. She was surrounded by friends, but society alone did not satisfy her. She always struggled each day to make Phoebe Apperson Hearst a greater woman. She also tried to make this a better world by softening its miseries, by aiding others in their endeavors. Her purse was always open to those in need, or to others endeavoring to educate themselves.

Doubtless this thirst for knowledge, this zeal in acquiring it, this ambition to aid those less fortunate than herself, was a great aid, not only to her husband, George

Hearst, but it left its stamp upon her son, William Randolph Hearst. He was born April 29, 1863, at the Stevenson Hotel. This was a quiet family hotel, and very popular. Here the Hearsts lived until they went to a big roomy house on Rincon Hill. George Hearst was very fond of children, and all his pride was centered in his boy, "Sonny" he called him, and in Puss, the boy's mother. No house was too good for them. For the next two years Phoebe Hearst devoted most of her time to her son, and George Hearst went back to the stormy Comstock, which was now in the new State of Nevada. The Nevada mines had recovered from the serious check caused by the Indian war. Once more the mills of the Ophir were reopened, and out poured gold and silver. This gold and silver tempted the mining privateers.

Litigation sprang up on the Comstock. In fact, there is always litigation where there are mines. William M. Stewart, afterward United States Senator from Nevada, received annually two hundred thousand dollars in fees as the principal attorney for the Ophir and several other mining companies. The first important mining suit in Nevada involved the Ophir, and the litigation cost one million and seventy thousand dollars. The mine was involved in thirty-seven suits. In twenty-eight of them the company was plaintiff, and in nine defendant.

The mining laws prevailing when quartz was first discovered were loose and indefinite. The first locations were taken as placer claims, and inadequately described. When it was known that the richest claims were on top of a ledge, they were relocated as quartz, the locators claiming all the "dips," "spurs," angles and variations. These "dips" and "spurs" made legal war. The first Nevada Legislature passed an act that action for the recovery of mining claims should not be maintained unless it was shown that the plaintiff or his assigns had been in possession of the ground for two years before the suit was brought, or since 1859, when the Comstock claims were taken. But this law was evaded. Suits were brought into California, where most of the corporations were organized, and where most of the mining cases were compromised.

Litigation always caused the stock to decline. During the winter of 1859 Ophir sold as high as twelve hundred dollars a share. In April 1860, it was offered on the street for six hundred. The decline was caused by the Burning Moscow Company locating on ground first claimed by the Ophir. This company asserted that their ledge was distinct from the Ophir, and maintained that it was twenty-three feet wide, and as rich as the Comstock. The Ophir brought suit to recover possession of the disputed ground. Cross-cuts were made by the Ophir Company opening into the works of the Burning Moscow. Judge Gordon N. Mott ordered the Burning Moscow to cease work until the arguments in the application for a permanent injunction had been decided. Judge Mott believed in the One Lode theory. While he held the office of judge, the Ophir was triumphant, and Burning Moscow declined in price. Judge James A. North succeeded Judge Mott in office.

North believed there were several smaller lodes instead of one great lode. Burning Moscow went up again. Ophir dropped. On October 23, 1863, soon after Hearst returned from Missouri, the Ophir skirmished underground for several days and assaulted the Moscow's works.

Philip Deidesheimer, superintendent of the Burning Moscow, caused the arrest of the Ophir's superintendent, with eighteen of his men, for riotous conduct. The Ophir men were released on bail, but a temporary injunction restrained them from working within the limits fixed by the Burning Moscow Company. The suit of the Ophir against the Burning Moscow was dismissed. Then the Ophir crashed from seventeen hundred and fifty dollars a share to eleven hundred and fifty.

The Ophir began a new suit in another district. Almost immediately exceedingly rich ore uncovered in the northern end of the Ophir carried the stock up five hundred dollars a share.

The problem was to find out which was the main ledge or the Mother Lode of which the Comstock was a spur. The Burning Moscow Company contended that it was the Virginia ledge. Secretly William H. Garrison had bought all the other interest on the Virginia ledge. He notified the Ophir in October 1862, that he would contest their title to the Comstock. This threat sent the Ophir stock down from three thousand to eighteen hundred dollars per share. The company compromised by paying from sixty thousand to one hundred thousand for Garrison's title. Already the Ophir Company had possession of four so-called ledges within a distance of fourteen hundred feet.

Four other ledges were alleged to exist within less than half that distance. One of these was the Burning Moscow, which was being harried by other companies as they harried the Ophir. In November 1863, the Burning Moscow consolidated all its enemies and united against the Ophir. Its capital stock was increased from less than half a million to three million. They began suit for the ejectment of the Ophir.

The decision was delayed because the question of

geology was perplexing. Only actual exploration of the disputed ledges could decide the litigation. By February 1864, the Burning Moscow was valueless compared with the Ophir, but the stock was kited up to eighty-two dollars before the end of October. Then it receded to twenty dollars. It was given another toss. Each share in the company changed hands three times during the month.

All this litigation retarded the mining industry, and the companies themselves were facing ruin. The Moscow stock fell to five dollars, with few buyers.

Then the Ophir owners secretly bought nearly three thousand shares, and got a controlling interest. But they were confronted with an assessment of fifteen dollars a share. They refused to pay it, and the Board of Directors advertised the stock for sale on the eighteenth of October.

On the afternoon preceding the sale, stockholders made an application to have the shares on the books of the Burning Moscow Company, which had its office in San Francisco, transferred to a single person. But the secretary refused to permit the transfer until the assessment was paid. The stockholders then tried to restrain the company from selling their stock. They applied to Federal Judge Sawyer of San Francisco for an injunction.

No injunction could be granted, because, by the California law, this was a day for the election of the judiciary. No sheriff could serve the writ. The sale went on. The Moscow Company bought in the stock at a low price. There were few bidders. The succeeding day an injunction was obtained restraining the transfer of the stock to other purchasers until the courts should determine the legality of the assessment sale.

The long contest ended a few days later by the Ophir surrendering the Burning Moscow's stock, and giving besides seven thousand five hundred dollars for the possession of that part of the Moscow claim which had been in dispute, and which was of no value except to establish a boundary.

Notwithstanding all the inactivity inevitable during this litigation, the Ophir during the first four years yielded fifteen million in gold and silver. While these underground and court battles were going on, Hearst bought shares in other mines. He owned a big block of the Gould and Curry stock. He expanded his activities. He prospected. Most of all this prospecting delighted him. His young wife was not happy until he would let her go with him and wear her brown merino dress. They went to remote parts of Nevada and Utah. They visited inaccessible valleys, and rode over steep trails to high peaks. Together they ate bacon, beans and pancakes smoking hot from a campfire. At last Phoebe Hearst was a real miner's wife.

Phoebe Hearst was not satisfied to be separated from her family. Nor were the Appersons content to be so far from their daughter and their grandson. Soon they came to the Rincon Hill house to pay their daughter a long visit. They saw California, and they were conquered. They could not go back to Missouri, but they must have a place in the Santa Clara Valley. Finally they found one between Alviso and Lawrence Station. There they lived and died. They are buried in San Jose.

From the beginning, Mrs. Hearst said she wished to live on Russian Hill. She never abandoned that idea. Why hide away from beauty by living on Rincon Hill because fashion decreed it as the quarter of San Francisco where one must live? George Hearst could not find a place on Russian Hill, but he compromised by purchasing a very attractive house, built by a Frenchman of taste, on Chestnut Street, where his bride could see all the majestic ships pass on the bay. The Hearsts were among the first to leave Rincon Hill and live near the bay.

In those days Hearst was rated as a millionaire. Then suddenly in 1864 his faith in his luck was shaken. The Ophir bonanza gave signs of being exhausted.

# THE NINETEENTH CHAPTER

During the early sixties in Virginia City, Hearst met many men who were afterward to become famous, or rich and powerful, in the United States. There was Sam Clemens (Mark Twain). Hearst and Sam were both Missourians. They called each other by their first names. They shared a rollicking sense of humor. In Washington, after Hearst was United States Senator, Mark Twain used to recall at dinner in the beautiful Hearst house how the Senator in Virginia City had a new "biled" shirt sent to his room for some important occasion. Mark Twain had no white shirt, and so he happened into Hearst's room and casually borrowed the one saved by Hearst for the festivities. With great glee Mark Twain related his appearance at the banquet in Hearst's "biled" shirt, while Hearst had to wear an ordinary one. With equal good-natured glee, Hearst answered, "That's so, Sam. And it's the only time you were ever well-dressed in your life."

In Virginia City, too, at this time, Hearst met James G. Fair, later United States Senator. To Hearst the

Senator was always Jim Fair. He and Fair for several years planned and worked together. Fair was the very able superintendent of the Ophir. Another able man was "Bill" Stewart, Hearst's attorney, later United States Senator. John W. Mackay was in Virginia City at that time, also just beginning his career as one of the most important mining men in the United States. At that time William Sharon, later United States Senator from Nevada, was managing the Bank of California in Virginia City. In fact, the great western mining world of the future was in Virginia City in the early sixties.

In 1865 a new interest came into the life of George Hearst. During his absence from San Francisco, he received a telegram saying that the Democrats had nominated him for the Assembly. He had not sought the nomination, nor had he known it was coming, and so he was greatly pleased. Hearst was always fond of politics. In Missouri as in the South, especially in this era, politics was the most absorbing topic of conversation and interest. When he was twenty-six years of age Hearst had gone as a delegate to the Missouri State Convention, but he never thought of political preferment in California. His friends in San Francisco carried on his fight, and he entered the California Legislature.

He was surprised at his election, because no year in California politics was quite as stormy as 1865, and he had belonged to the LeCompton party, the party of Gwin and Terry. In April of 1865 came the fall of Richmond and the surrender of Lee. When this event was celebrated, business was suspended. Hot, feverish patriotism showed itself in parades, fireworks and conviviality. There were about the same number of Democrats in San Francisco as Republicans, so the political contest of 1865 was very keen. The assassination of Lincoln brought profound gloom and general disorder. To be a Democrat was almost to be under suspicion as a "rebel." A San Francisco gang destroyed presses and scattered type in the offices of the Democratic press, the *Occidental*, the *News Letter* and the *Monitor*.

The political struggle was so keen at the Sacramento convention that warring factions assailed one another with hickory canes, cuspidors, ink stands and chair legs. Out of that convention came three candidates for the United States Senate, Cornelius Cole, A. A. Sargent, and John D. Felton.

All winter the political storm continued. The weather was the worst known in the history of the state, and never was there so much conflict in the Legislature. Young Mrs. Hearst was only twenty-three, and she was unaware of what life would be as the wife of a California legislator. At that time wintering in Sacramento, and being a member of the Legislature, were taken more seriously than now. It was with a flutter of pride that Mrs. Hearst packed her big trunks and set out with her small boy from her pleasant house on Chestnut Street for a winter at the capital. With her went Miss Camilla Price, her companion and friend.

The Sacramento steamer sailed at four o'clock in the afternoon. There was always a flurry of excitement at the dinner hour, and the evening was like a political reception. The capital, with its palms, camellias and handsome building of state, looked very imposing to the young wife. She began to wonder if her husband would not become a real statesman at Washington.

The sixteenth session of the California Legislature convened at Sacramento on the fourth of December 1865.

The Unionists were in control of both houses. In the Senate were thirty-one Unionists; in the Assembly sixty-one. There were nineteen Democrats in the Assembly, and nine in the Senate. The San Francisco legislators were men who afterward became more or less famous. The Senators from San Francisco and San Mateo Counties were: A. L. Tubbs, William J. Shaw, H. L. Dodge, Horace Hawes and J. S. Hager. The Assemblymen were: Charles Clayton, James Bowman, C. L. Wiggin, S. E. Bagbee, Henry Dutton, G. A. McClelland, M. A. Braley, Michael Hawkins, George Hearst, Samuel L. Lupton and E. J. Chase. Other Senators were P. Banning of Los Angeles; David Belden of Nevada; John P. Jones of Shasta and Trinity; L. B. Mizner of Solano and Yolo. Governor Low opened the war by sending an inflammatory message to the Senate. He said that Virginia's motto had been: "The ignorance of the many promotes the well-being of the few"—while Massachusetts from her infancy, proclaimed to the world "the great truth that knowledge is power."

In an impassioned address Senator Mizner denounced the Governor's statement as uncalled for, illiberal and an insult to those representing a certain section of the Union. He hurled at the Puritans, "Salem witchcraft!"

Trouble was avoided in the Assembly because that body read perfunctorily the opening paragraphs of the Governor's message, and then ordered it to be printed.

As soon as the Senate was called to order, Lieutenant-Governor Machin made an eloquent speech on the "downfall of the rebellion." Shaw of San Francisco placed before the Senate for ratification the amendment to the constitution abolishing slavery forever within the limits of the republic. Shaw was a Democrat, and this move caused a tremendous sensation. The Senate passed the resolution with only four dissenting voices: J. W. Freeman of Fresno and Tulare; Warren S. Montgomery of Mariposa, Merced and Stanislaus; George Pearce of Sonoma; and John A. Rush of Colusa and Tehama.

Thomas Eager of Alameda, a Unionist, offered the ratification resolution in the Assembly. It was passed by a vote of sixty-six to eleven. The eleven Democrats opposing it were: A. C. Bledsoe of Sonoma; J. L. Dowling of Sonoma; John B. Goodin of Lassen and Plumas; George Hearst of San Francisco; O. A. Hoag of Sonoma; William Holden of Mendocino; William S. Long of Colusa and Tehama; R. P. Mace of Fresno; E. C. Parrish of Los Angeles; John W. Satterwhite of San Bernardino; and R. H. Ward of Merced and Stanislaus. They were all Democrats. Only one of them, Mace of Fresno, returned to Sacramento to serve in the next session of the Legislature.

Those voting against ratification were attacked with the bitterness of invective engendered by war. They were caricatured and it was thought cast into political oblivion.

When the Senate and the Assembly met in joint convention to elect a United States Senator the supporters of Sargent presented the only serious opposition to Cornelius Cole, but they could not muster enough strength, and Sargent retired. Cole was elected with a total of ninety-two votes. The Democrats gave William T. Coleman, famous leader of the Vigilantes, twenty-six complimentary votes and Eugene Casserly, one. Hearst voted for Coleman.

During the rest of the winter George Hearst served on the Assembly committee of Mines and Mining Interests. He studied the State's Geological Survey, and the committee report of commendation that followed had an important bearing on the future of that work. He attended a meeting of miners held in San Francisco, January 1866, voted to endorse the recently organized mining bureau and was a delegate to the State Convention of Miners that met in Sacramento shortly afterward.

In general, Hearst worked and voted for the interests of San Francisco as he understood them. On measures of political complexion he acted in concert with the rest of the Democratic minority. He voted according to his convictions. Wherever he was, he was always himself, and that Emerson calls one test of greatness. When the Legislature adjourned Hearst was glad. He was restless away from the mines. He missed the great game in Nevada. When he returned to San Francisco he thought his political career was finished, and Mrs. Hearst feared that her husband would never be a Washington statesman.

# THE TWENTIETH CHAPTER

Soon after the close of the Civil War, Hearst was discouraged by the business slump in the United States. In addition to the financial depression, all the gold ore in sight in the ledges of the Ophir seemed worked out. Hearst had bought a part interest in several locations and mines, borrowing whenever he thought it feasible in order to extend his holdings. In one transaction he lost four hundred thousand dollars. Suddenly he found he could borrow no more. Overnight, property was apparently valueless.

When the rumors spread that the Ophir bonanza had suddenly played out, the mining industry on the Comstock was paralyzed. If the Ophir was exhausted, what hope was there for Nevada? Doubtless that was what George Hearst said when in 1867 he turned his erect back squarely on the Comstock. He thought he was done with mining forever, and with everything in Nevada. He was as discouraged as an optimistic, resilient nature can be.

Hearst was forty-seven years of age when he came

down from Nevada to San Francisco to begin life all over again. He was tall, erect, rugged, with a broad brow, a well-formed high head, a striking aquiline nose and a long, graying pioneer's beard. He was slow-moving. He always wore a slouch hat down over his eyes, and on his feet were high-topped boots. He usually wore a cutaway coat, and occasionally, with great reluctance, he appeared in a frock coat.

Luckily Hearst had bought real estate in San Francisco, and this investment showed considerable activity. For two years after he had left the Comstock, he purchased and sold real estate with such shrewdness that at the end of that time he had made one hundred and sixty thousand dollars. Gains from real estate to Hearst never seemed real money. Buying and selling property palled on him. The city was not his "game." In town he was restless, circumscribed, thwarted, half-alive, like a big ship with no ocean. Always his thoughts turned to mountains and mines.

Hearst borrowed thirty thousand dollars on some property in San Francisco, invested it in a mine in Kern County, and made considerable money out of the venture. In this way he became acquainted with James W. Haggin and his brother-in-law, Lloyd Tevis, who had baronial interests there. Hearst's Kern County experience renewed his feeling that for him metals were no mystery and no gamble. He knew so much about the formation of the earth that at his touch the earth seemed to give forth silver and gold. His confidence in himself as a miner grew, and also his courage in chance-taking.

From this time on Hearst did not make his own locations. He would not tie himself down to one property, nor would he manage mines, though later he controlled the administration of many. Rapidly he found his most important function, that of a mining expert. Often he was paid as high as fifty thousand dollars for his opinion of a mine. He was an expert, prepared to back his own judgment. When he approved of a property, he was willing to buy—at his own price. At his own price also he was usually willing to sell to those who thought they saw in a mine more value than he did.

George Hearst now began to range all over the mining districts of western America. Youth and its enthusiasm seemed to have come back. His horses and mules traveled over desolate deserts. He listened to the deadly hiss of the rattler hiding under sun-baked rocks. He scrambled through hot canyons. He toiled up heat-seared mountains. He slept under frosty stars.

Hearst was never so happy as when his wife went with him. The dainty, exquisite woman with a face like a dream of da Vinci had become a real miner's wife. Always on these trips of investigation and exploration the Hearsts were companioned by men with leathery, tanned cheeks and whose eyes held the far-seeing look that penetrates rocks and earth. Once they climbed a slope of Mount Tenabo, an isolated peak of the Toiyabe Range in central Nevada. Hearst acquired a controlling interest in the Simeon Wenban silver locations, but unsettled conditions deterred him from developing the property. He resold to Wenban for fourteen thousand dollars. Hearst's Tenabo locations included the Garrison and other mines that founded the Wenban fortune.

Hearst invested ninety thousand dollars with James G. Fair and some of those "Comstock fellows," as he spoke of them, in a so-called El Dorado in Idaho. He lost his ninety thousand dollars. In Idaho he was offered an attractive "salted" mine. It had been artistically "salted," and looked entrancingly rich. When he inspected mining properties Hearst used one of his coat pockets as a sample bag. The offered samples Hearst recognized as too rich to be true. Secretly Hearst managed to get samples other than those shown. Assays proved that the mine was "salted," and the owners afterward admitted it. Hearst didn't denounce them. He simply didn't buy the mine. He spared the feelings of the promoters, but he was not victimized. Hearst did not linger in Idaho. The territory never gave him the "lucky" feeling that he had in Nevada.

Bleak, dusty, sun-scorched, alkali desert, Nevada, with its coyotes and its rattlers lurking in sagebrush and greasewood, never failed to flash him a summons. There came to him promising reports from the Mineral Hill districts in the mountains between Elko and Eureka. Investigation destroyed Hearst's interest in the property. Other experts made a different report, and an English company lost a million dollars in Mineral Hill.

James B. Haggin, with whom Hearst became acquainted in Kern County mining ventures followed Hearst's work and noted his unerring judgment. He sensed that George Hearst was a mining genius. Haggin was a Turkish-American lawyer, who looked like a sultan and had a subtle, Oriental intuition about people. He found out that Hearst never betrayed friend or trust. This was the kind of a man Haggin desired as an associate; he told Hearst to count on him for investments.

From Mineral Hill, Hearst traveled fifty trying miles to Eureka, in southeastern Nevada. This camp is at an altitude of sixty-five hundred feet. Ore was first discovered there in 1864, but the claims were abandoned because they were not rich enough. In Eureka, Hearst found that B. E. Buell and Isaac Bateman had consolidated a number of valuable claims which they were willing to sell for a million dollars. These mines produced one-third gold and two-thirds silver. Hearst wrote to some San Francisco associates, William Thompson, George D. Roberts and others, that the prospects were good. They urged that the mine be bought. The partners put up four hundred thousand dollars, and gave a mortgage for the rest. Hearst contributed forty thousand dollars lent him by James B. Haggin. He and his partners were paid eighty thousand dollars as experts.

The Eureka ores were "rebellious." Old-time miners did not like them, but C. A. Stetefeldt and Colonel G. C. Robbins introduced a process of handling the ore that was recognized by Hearst as a great advance. The outcome more than justified his judgment. The Eureka Consolidated, Richmond Consolidated, and Ruby Consolidated, between 1869 and 1883 produced forty million dollars of silver, twenty million dollars of gold, and two hundred and twenty-five thousand tons of lead. Between 1871 and 1881 the Eureka alone had a gross yield of nineteen million and paid over five million in dividends.

The Eureka district also produced the famous contest between the Eureka and the Richmond. This was the first "apex suit" in mining history. It began in 1877, and was won by the Eureka Consolidated in 1881. It was tried in San Francisco before Stephen J. Field, Justice of the United States Supreme Court, United States District Judge Lorenzo Sawyer and E. W. Hillyer, United States District Judge of Nevada. For the plaintiff appeared Solomon Heydenfeldt, R. S. Mesick, John Barber and H. J. Thornton. The defendant was represented by

S. M. Wilson, Thomas Wren and J. J. Williams. Hearst had no patience with this litigation. "Those inside got to quarreling," he said, "they said we were stalling. I got mad and sold out."

Then Hearst went over to Pioche Ridge in southeastern Nevada. Pioche is a mining town at an elevation of five thousand, seven hundred and twenty-five feet. It was named for F. L. A. Pioche, a San Francisco banker, who sent a representative there to buy claims in 1868. In the following year W. H. Raymond and John H. Ely relocated a number of abandoned claims under the name of the Raymond and Ely Mine. A stampede to Pioche was on. In 1872 the town had a population of six thousand men and several hundred women. From 1870 to 1875 the district produced sixteen million in gold, silver, lead and zinc. The Raymond and Ely had a yield at that time of over seven million dollars, and paid in dividends two million, six hundred and eighty-five thousand dollars. The Meadow Valley also proved a great producer.

Hearst was rather apologetic about the little he accomplished in Pioche. "I didn't do much," he said, "just knocked around a little. Got in with some men who had a set of Pioche mines, sunk a shaft, struck a bed of ore, had a big lawsuit over it, got out of that making two hundred and fifty thousand."

Sam Davis, in his history of Nevada, tells us an amusing story of this litigation. Davis' stories are seldom literally true, but doubtless this one is characteristic of the bench and bar in those days. Davis says that Cinc Barnes, a smart lawyer, drifted into Pioche. The Raymond and Ely Mine was contiguous to the Hermes Mine, a property of which George Hearst was part owner. Hearst was absent in another part of Nevada, but Barnes told the other owners that the Raymond and Ely people were stealing their ore. He advised a suit, and his counsel was taken. Then he went to the Raymond and Ely Company and called the Hermes crowd blackmailers. Barnes was employed by both sides, and he made the jury think that each side thought the case favorably "fixed." The stock market responded, and Barnes and his gang bought heavily.

When the case was over the jury retired for deliberation. A rope was lowered from the jury room window and hauled back carrying a boot full of gold marked Raymond and Ely. This operation was repeated several times, the golden boot sometimes bearing the name Raymond and Ely and sometimes Hermes. Davis says the jury proceeded to "weigh the evidence." Hermes evidence outweighed that sent up by Raymond and Ely, and Hermes won the suit. Barnes and his conspirators are said to have cleaned up a large fortune. It is true that there was a suit of Hermes vs. Raymond and Ely, but the Hermes lost.

About this time Hearst and Haggin formed a mining partnership. They had two rules: one was, never buy an interest in a mine or shares in a property controlled by others; the other was, never give more for a mine than the value of ore in sight. Hearst and Haggin bought an entire property and managed it themselves. Occasionally they sold an interest or ten percent to their superintendent or to the public, but control was kept in their own hands.

When owners wishing to sell urged that the invisible supply was probably greater than the visible, Hearst would reply: "That's why we are willing to buy. If there is no more ore in your mine than we see, we shall make a bad bargain if we pay you the value of what we can't see. We look to the invisible supply for our profit. We don't urge you to sell, but we don't invest on any other terms."

This system founded the success of the firm of Hearst and Haggin. The first great mine acquired under this partnership was the Ontario in Utah.

# THE TWENTY-FIRST CHAPTER

IN 1872 Hearst was told that in Utah there was an opportunity to buy the "biggest mine in the world." This information was given him in a confidential telegram, but he did not get excited. With ever increasing frequency he was told confidentially about a new "biggest mine in the world."

Hearst was now fifty-two, and he had come to be considered the greatest living mining expert. His analyses of mines were quoted in European mining schools. Prospectors followed him around as if he were a magician whose footsteps led to success, and the touch of whose hands turned earth to gold. He was listened to like a prophet.

At the time George Hearst was told of this new "biggest mine in the world" he was spending the summer in Salt Lake City, always on the trail of a new discovery. Lincoln said that Utah would prove to be the treasure house of the nation, and Brigham Young declared that there was enough gold in Utah to pave the streets of the new Jerusalem. But Young did not encourage mining among Mormons as he did agriculture. "We cannot eat gold and silver," he said.

In 1863 General Conner headed a movement to develop Utah's mines. This movement continued until 1872 when George Hearst was asked to examine some mining prospects in the forbidding canyons of the Wasatch Mountains. He had been especially asked to investigate the McHenry Mine. It had been bonded in San Francisco. George Hearst looked over the McHenry property, but he found it far from answering the description of being "the biggest mine in the world." He turned his back on it and returned to Salt Lake City.

While in Utah he met Marcus Daly at a place called Lake Flat. Marcus Daly was boss foreman for W. A. Clark, ever on the lookout for new mines. Salt Lake City was his headquarters. At Lake Flat Daly told Hearst about a prospect just seen by him near what is now Park City, in the Uintah District. Daly said his employers did not like it, but he thought Hearst might. He described it as a little hole in the ground of about four feet.

Uintah is the name of an Indian tribe. The district is in the western Weber canyon. This canyon had been explored in 1776 by Spaniards who came up from Santa Fe.

Hearst went over to look at the "little hole in the ground" in the Uintah District. It was only about half a mile off his trail. He found a hole as deep as a man's shoulders and six feet long. It was sunk around the side of a vein. Hearst looked at it and dug away a little earth. One of the owners standing on the bank said: "Tear that down all you want to."

Hearst dug down farther. Then the man said: "I've had a chance to make a stake and go home three times since I came here. I must get some money out of this thing. I'm going to sell."

This owner was a Canadian, Herman Budden. Together with a Missourian named Rector Steen and other miners, John Kain and Gus McDowell, he owned the mine. These men had prospected for a long time without any great success in these remote hills, thirty-five miles southeast of Salt Lake, beyond a mountain barrier. Finally they located a claim more than a mile up the canyon from Parley's Peak, or Park City, in Wasatch County. One day Budden, in going to his claim, automatically struck his pick into the rock along the trail. Something flew up that attracted his attention. He went back and examined the outcropping. It was chloride. That careless touch of the pick served him well. He had struck a bit of rock about the size of a hat protruding a few inches from the ground—the only outcropping of the lode. He dug and found rich silver ore. He and his partners called it the Ontario. They started to prospect by sinking a hole and running a cut on the side of the lode.

Hearst looked over the claim carefully and asked Budden how much he wanted. "Twenty-five thousand dollars," was the answer. Hearst thought even that hole in the ground was worth it, but he replied that not much work had been done. "Well," answered Budden, "there isn't much done yet, but stay around here and watch us. I'm going to sell."

There was a big rush on to Pioche. Some of Hearst's associates came the next morning to wake him, and urge him to go to Pioche.

"No," he said, "I'm going to stay right here and watch this little mine."

Hearst waited three weeks while another hole was sunk. More rock was taken out. Hearst took some, and had it sampled at Salt Lake City. It assayed from one hundred to four hundred ounces of silver to the ton, with by-products of lead, zinc, copper and gold. Without waiting further, on August 21, 1872, he decided to give Budden and his associates twenty-seven thousand dollars. He paid three thousand to another man who claimed to have an interest.

The Ontario Mine was the first of the great mines purchased and developed by Hearst and Haggin. R. C. Chambers was made resident manager, and given an interest in the company. It was a small interest, but it made him a millionaire. The Ontario Mine was the foundation of Hearst's great permanent fortune.

Hearst remained at the Ontario Mine to organize a plan of development, but all the time he kept on prospecting. The Ontario was hard to work because the character of the ore was difficult. It had to be worked very "close." The silver was uniform. The cost of mining and milling was thirty-four dollars a ton. The rock produced on an average of one hundred and six dollars a ton. The second year, Hearst rented a mill, and after that he built a large mill. There were sixty miles of underground workings, with a drain tunnel two miles long through which rushed a torrent drained from a large area rich in minerals.

In the first ten years the Ontario was developed to a depth of eight hundred feet. The vein was of quartzite formation, with a pay-chute several hundred feet long and twenty-three feet wide. The Ontario was one of the deepest mines in the world, and one of the most productive. This mine established the Salt Lake City Valley as one of the largest smelting centers in the world. At the close of 1883 the total output of the Ontario was more than seventeen million. Dividends of six million, two hundred and fifty thousand dollars had been distributed.

The "roasting ore" of the Ontario was expensive to work. Hearst was obliged to purchase furnaces, and a forty stamp mill. A Cornish pumping machine at the mine was installed at a depth of two thousand feet. About a million dollars were expended before the mine began to yield profit. Yet in 1872 to the end of 1876 the Ontario netted one million, one hundred thousand dollars. In December 1876, it was incorporated, and from this time its dividend record is available. From 1877 to 1891, the year of George Hearst's death, the Ontario paid dividends of twelve million, four hundred and twenty-five thousand dollars.

While Hearst was developing the Ontario he continued to look for more prospects. He bought another mine, the Daly. After this mine was put on its feet, it produced thirty thousand dollars a month. Hearst bought mine after mine. He did not worry about funds, but the development of the Ontario and the Daly made him stagger under the burden. He always said it took a mine to make a mine.

While Hearst was living at the Ontario Mine in 1873, he found that he would be absent from home for nearly a year. So Mrs. Hearst rented the Chestnut Street house, and took their son William Randolph, now a boy of ten, on her long dreamed of and carefully planned trip to Europe.

William Randolph Hearst had gone to public schools, and he was glad to see the countries he had studied about in geography. On their way to Europe Mrs. Hearst and her son visited their relations in Missouri and went on to New York, Washington and Boston. Mrs. Hearst kept a diary, and every night she made a record of the day. She also wrote a letter to her husband. She touched George Hearst when, in a letter, she told him that the poor classes in Ireland were so poor that Willie wanted to give away all his money and clothes. The sight of another boy of the age of his own absent child, "Sonny Boy," caused Hearst to do many kindnesses for other children. He wrote back to his wife that we was "very lonely with no boy."

The travelers visited England, Scotland, and the Continent, while George Hearst wrestled with the difficulty of putting two mines on their feet.

Hearst was glad when his wife and son came back in 1874, but Mrs. Hearst and William Randolph did not return to the same San Francisco they had left. It was not even the same America. The country was sick. All America had been in too great a hurry to get rich. Thousands thought they were rich. They bought extravagant luxuries. They spent dream money, and now they were paying for it. A panic was on. Everyone seemed bankrupt, Mackay, Fair, and even Con Virginia were tottering. Hearst had to have money, and more money, and more money to develop the Ontario and the Daly. He sold everything salable to put into those mines. He knew that they were as safe as the mint. He would stake his reputation, his future, the future of his wife and son on them.

Mrs. Hearst helped. She sold the Chestnut Street home, the home that looked out on the bay with the ships passing from morning until night. She gave up her horses and carriages. She discharged her servants and went with her husband and son to live at a boarding house. In that boarding house she made some of her best friends, for she was a real woman, and she recognized real people. She bore defeat as she bore success, with a smile. She was a fitting mate for George Hearst, the pioneer.

# THE TWENTY-SECOND CHAPTER

George and Phoebe Hearst retrenched in expenditures for one year, and once more money came out of its hole and appeared in California. The Ontario Mine paid dividends. It was incorporated, and fifty thousand of the one hundred and fifty thousand shares were sold at fifteen dollars a share. For several years it paid seventy-five thousand a month. From the Ontario and the Daly Mines success swept like a tidal wave to George Hearst. He was now fifty-five. From the far Black Hills in Dakota there came to Hearst another call of gold.

The Black Hills gold rush came about accidentally. One of Custer's soldiers found gold July 31, 1874. General Custer was sent in 1874 to explore the Sioux reservation in the Black Hills region. Custer's force camped near French Creek. Private William McKay of Custer's company was an old miner. He panned out rich gold and told the General. Custer reported the discovery to army headquarters at St. Paul. The news spread like a forest fire. A new diggings, Custer City, was born.

In the late fall of 1875 rich placer diggings were discovered in Deadwood Gulch. Custer City became a "ghost town," and Deadwood arose almost overnight. Then the Sioux went on the warpath. Crazy Horse, Black Moon and Sitting Bull were "making medicine" against the white men. Custer took the field, and on June 26, 1876, Custer's force was wiped out at the Little Big Horn.

Meanwhile, for a year miners had clamored to get into the Black Hills country. As early as August 1875, in Salt Lake, Hearst had seen a sample of the Black Hills gold. He took it and had it assayed. He tried to send the Ontario superintendent, Chambers, to the Black Hills, but no one cared to venture into Deadwood Gulch with the Sioux on the warpath.

Then a San Francisco mining man, John Sevenoaks, made his way into Deadwood Gulch after the Custer Massacre and got hold of a mine. He telegraphed Hearst about it, even spending four hundred dollars on telegrams. Hearst was very ill at the time, and he didn't read Sevenoak's telegrams until he recovered. He knew that Sevenoaks was an able mining man, and he was impressed by his enthusiasm. Hearst telegraphed Chambers at the Ontario to send William A. Farish to look over this Black Hills Mine. Farish did not share Sevenoaks' enthusiasm, but he lingered for a time in the Black Hills country. Finally he telegraphed that he had a good thing. Hearst telegraphed him at once to get a bond on the mine, and this he did.

Soon it became known in San Francisco that George Hearst had asked a representative to bond a certain mine, and some capitalists on Montgomery Street tried to get shares in the new enterprise. When it came to financing the venture these capitalists revealed that they wanted the whole mine or nothing.

Hearst placed the situation before James B. Haggin. At first Haggin shook his head saying: "Deadwood is too far away. I don't want it."

Then Hearst said to Haggin: "I'm going to the Black Hills tomorrow morning."

Haggin knew that Hearst would not take that long trying trip, and double back on the Overland Trail of 1850, unless he was certain that the prospect was unusually good. He agreed to abide by Hearst's judgment. Hearst made preparations for immediate departure. There was little time to lose because the bond would expire within three days after he could possibly reach Deadwood Gulch.

Mrs. Hearst had lived through several panics. She knew that the Ontario and the Daly Mines established the family future in comfort and luxury. She rather dreaded new, unnecessary ventures. Her big, stalwart husband was forever setting out for far mountains and desert lands with valises full of clothing, and coming back with valises full of rocks and quartz, samples of his newest mines. When she saw him making ready to leave for Deadwood Gulch, Dakota, she had a little apprehensive shudder at the hazard, so she said: "George, if you find a good mine, let's have it as a homestake."

"Puss, we will," answered her husband. "We'll call it the Homestake Mine." So before it was born, the Homestake was christened.

Hearst journeyed to the lawless land of Deadwood, the "wickedest town on earth," where Wild Bill Hickok and Calamity Jane reigned. Hearst had seen too many "wickedest towns on earth" to be interested in another shooting, fighting camp. He rapidly rode out to the gulch south of Deadwood.

He arrived in time, but his bond had only three days to run, and he was obliged to have quick action. Some capitalists on Montgomery Street had promised that the purchase money would be waiting for him on his arrival in Deadwood. There was no money. Luckily, he had only half-counted on the capitalists, and he had carried with him to Dakota a large sum of money. The mine was all that he expected, and he bought a good share for eighty thousand dollars.

At first the Homestake was chaos. During Hearst's absence a shaft was sunk thirty feet at a cost of thirty thousand dollars. When Hearst came back to Deadwood he dismissed the superintendent and placed in charge a man named McMaster. Then he telegraphed Haggin that they must either sell all, or buy control. The Homestake was a huge mine, and of low grade. It must be worked cheaply, on a great scale, or it would fail. Haggin telegraphed Hearst to buy control.

Before the season was over, Hearst had organized the great Homestake Mine. In a little more than a year after the Custer Massacre, he bought all the side claims. The Homestake Mining Company came from the consolidation of the ground and equipment of the Father de Smet Consolidated Gold Mining Company, the Deadwood Terra Mining Company, the Caledonia Gold Mining Company, the Highland Mining Company. These mines are near the town of Lead, Lawrence County, South Dakota.

Hearst and Haggin bought in all two hundred and fifty claims or two thousand, six hundred and sixteen acres. At the surface were several veins. Three united deeper down. The main vein ranged from three hundred to five hundred feet in width. The first mill of eighty stamps began crushing ore July 12, 1878. Another mill of one hundred and twenty stamps, the Golden Star, crushed ore in 1879. From December, 1879, the Homestake paid dividends. During twenty years more than eighty million were mined with gold bearing veins at one thousand feet depth widening in the lower levels. In 1899 enough ore was exposed to keep busy mills of five thousand tons daily capacity for twenty-five years. In 1899 the Homestake led in the production of gold ore in the United States.

On the Comstock, ore which ran below twenty dollars a ton was left in the mine or thrown on the dump. Much Homestake ore did not average more than three dollars and fifty cents a ton, but there was a mountain of it to be chewed up by great machines. It could be quarried rather than mined. Equipment for its concentration was almost perfect. Nearly all sulphides were saved. Only five percent of all material down to eight hundred and fifty feet yielded four dollars a ton, but Hearst so skillfully treated huge masses at one time with a great number of stamps that the mine was worked profitably. Any ore that had even two dollars a ton could be worked without loss. Hearst installed machinery until there were six hundred stamps running.

In addition to the large sums obtained from the mine itself Hearst and Haggin acquired water rights which supplied water for the stamp mills and also neighboring towns. These water rights cost one hundred and seventy thousand dollars, but during Hearst's lifetime they yielded nearly one hundred thousand a year. The Homestake Company built a railroad which brought wood to the mine and served the rapidly increasing population. The railroad earned fifteen thousand dollars a month. Hearst and Haggin constructed lumber mills, stores, commissaries. The pay roll was extensive enough to support the entire City of Lead. A community was created.

Phoebe Hearst felt that Homestake was her own child. She had christened the mine. She founded the Hearst Free Library and the Hearst Free Kindergarten. She often visited the kindergarten and gave suggestions to the teachers and gifts to the pupils. When she came, the teachers and children felt happier for her visit.

After George Hearst grew rich as a result of his many fortunate investments, his San Francisco secretary complained that he couldn't keep him supplied with money. He used to set out from his office in San Francisco with his pockets full of twenty dollar gold pieces, but he seldom had enough money to reach home. Up and down Montgomery Street he was accosted by old prospectors. They were in bad luck and they begged a loan. George Hearst never gave less than a twenty dollar gold piece. Very frequently he grubstaked his old friends. Down-and-outers were never forgotten by him. He tided over many a miner with a loan. He and his friends always called each other by their first names. When it was suggested to him that he gave to the unworthy, his reply was: "Oh, well, they are my old mining pals. I struck it rich. They didn't. They might have been lucky. So I ought to divide."

# THE TWENTY-THIRD CHAPTER

AFTER Hearst organized and developed the Home-stake Mine his footsteps in the western mining world led from Dakota to the Cordillera. Often his assays of mines were quoted in schools of mines. He was considered the best judge of mines in the world. He was so much in demand, his judgment was so often sought, that he had scarcely any private life. From the time of his great success he belonged largely to his career. William Randolph Hearst recalled him as always going and coming with valises full of quartz specimens.

In his early sixties Hearst was called "Uncle George" by many who loved him. He was a striking figure, with a long, white beard and fine, deep-seeing eyes. He was always erect. He walked with deliberation. He spoke with judgment and dignity. He never chattered, nor made unnecessary remarks, but he liked to be surrounded by cheery, amiable, diverting people. He listened well. He seldom led conversation, but frequently, when a significant remark was made, suddenly his eyes would light up, and he would flash humorous comment.

As he grew older, at times his manner appeared distrait. He seemed not to listen. In reality, he was empire-building. Often he sat at the table, crumbling bread with his sensitive, long fingers, while his eyes were faraway in Mexico, Idaho, Arizona, Nevada, Dakota, Montana. Robert Turner, the Hearsts' colored butler who was with them for thirty-five years, would brush away the crumbs, and get his employer a fresh piece of bread. Hearst would continue crumbling the bread, wholly unconscious that he had a new portion. He was still in the Black Hills or the Cordillera.

After the Civil War, the Hearsts' house was constantly filled with guests, many of them having lost their fortunes in the war. The Hearsts appeared to have entertained most of Franklin County, and much of St. Louis. No tale of unhappiness wearied George or Phoebe Hearst, and no trouble was ever told in the Hearst house to indifferent ears. Phoebe Hearst recalled Missouri, when schools were scattered. She was always helping kindergartens, artists, musicians, writers, and pretty, poor girls who needed a home or background. She made many matches, and bought many trousseaus.

After leaving the Chestnut Street house, the Hearsts lived in boarding houses and at the Grand Hotel, and later bought, remodeled and refurnished handsomely the large Graves house on Van Ness Avenue. The Graves house was sold, and in the eighties they occupied the Addison Head house on Taylor Street. George Hearst came home from his long journeys gratefully to preside at his wife's side in the dining room. He looked taller seated than standing. At the foot of the table sat "Cousin Joe" Clark, who was a member of the family. Cousin Joe was fine looking, wore smart English clothes, had a gay, engaging manner, made many witty retorts, and told endless amusing stories. In the early days Cousin Joe had turned over to George Hearst some money for investment. The transaction was not a success, but the order at the Hearst office was that Cousin Joe should have whatever he asked. Cousin Joe was a part of the Hearst household until he died, in 1900.

Another friend of Hearst's at this time was Jasper MacDonald, whose wife was one of Mrs. Hearst's protégées, and who lived with the family for years. Mr. and Mrs. Jasper MacDonald were married in the Hearst house. William M. Lent, with whom Hearst was associated in real estate in San Francisco in the sixties, continued his friendship. Hearst's attorney, Clarence Greathouse of Kentucky, who was later Privy Councilor to the King of Siam, was also a friend. Colonel A. E. Head was a friend from Nevada City days, and Captain Lloyd Rawlings was a Virginia City friend, who was associated with Hearst in several enterprises. Captain Rawlings managed the Durango property for twenty-five years. Thomas J. Grier, the superintendent of the Homestake Mine, and R. C. Chambers, superintendent of the Ontario, were Hearst's close friends. Samuel Strauss, Mark Twain, Marcus Daly, and Senator Stanford, where also friends of Hearst's.

Little things never disturbed Hearst. He did not like to be bothered with details. He was always thinking of great projects, huge mines, mountain ranges in the sky, land by the hundreds of thousands of acres. If he had lived long enough, he would have been an oil king because his exploration of the earth's interior showed him that underground were seas of oil in California.

Haggin was like Hearst in his range of interests. They plunged together. Haggin was a lawyer, but he was fascinated by mines. Hearst and Haggin lost in Bodie mines nine hundred thousand dollars. At Custer, Idaho, they made one hundred and twenty-five thousand dollars, but in their other Idaho ventures they lost heavily. In the Mexican mining district of Durango they had one of their notable successes.

The San Luis Mine, about one hundred and fifty miles from Mazatlan, in San Dimas, Durango, gave the Hearsts for many years twenty-five thousand dollars a month profit. The gold and silver ore was packed out on mule-back. After the mine was held up by bandits, the gold and silver ore, in the time of Diaz, was escorted to Mazat-lan by a guard of seventy men. Mrs. Rawlings, wife of Captain Rawlings, who for many years had charge of the mine, told of going to the San Luis Mine by stage and muleback, and fording a river one hundred and fifty-two times. Now airplanes go to the San Luis Mine in a short time.

Eighteen hundred and eighty-one came and with it George Hearst's last great mining achievement. He had worked in lead, gold, silver and zinc, and now he plunged into a new, unknown medium, and made his greatest success. He thought he was investing in a silver mine, but it was characteristic of the flood of fortune always flowing toward him that the silver mine should prove to be one of the greatest copper mines the world has ever seen, the Anaconda.

Like the Ontario, the Anaconda came to Hearst's attention through Marcus Daly. Daly knew mines. He represented the Walker Brothers of Salt Lake City in Butte, Montana. He had great faith in a silver prospect on Anaconda Hill. He tried to interest the Walker Brothers, but they doubted his judgment. He left them, and went to work for himself. At this time Daly called on Hearst for help. He wrote him that he had bonded the silver mine on Anaconda Hill, near Butte. The mine had been prospected only, and there was no telling how it would pan out.

"If you will come with me," Daly added, "I will take a quarter interest, or whatever you say."

Hearst had confidence in Marcus Daly who was a working foreman. He handed his letter to Haggin, and asked him to write Daly. Then he went away to a mine in Arizona.

Shortly afterward, in a telegraph office on the Arizona desert, Hearst was handed a message. This telegram said that Daly had made other arrangements. Hearst had only Daly's guess about the value of the mine, but the description of it aroused his interest so much that he telegraphed immediately to Daly apologizing for Haggin's neglect in answering the letter. He promised to go in with him.

Daly telegraphed back that he had made arrangements with W. A. Clark, later United States Senator from Montana. Hearst telegraphed Daly to buy out Clark. Daly answered that he could get back a quarter. Hearst telegraphed him to buy that quarter.

Hearst bought a quarter interest in the Anaconda Mine without ever having seen it. Then he went to Montana to look it over.

In 1864, placer gold was discovered by an emigrant in what is now Main Street in Butte, Montana. That same year quartz veins were located by miners from California. Silver was found in 1865. Butte was born in 1866. The district enjoyed great prosperity until 1868, when the miners sought more promising fields. Copper mining had been attempted in 1866, but the smelting was unsuccessful. In 1872, William A. Clark gave first serious attention to the copper mines of the district. Once more Butte became a lively camp. In 1879, Clark promoted the construction of a custom mill, and Butte grew to city size. As yet nobody, not even Daly, suspected that there was copper ore on Anaconda Hill, west of the town.

When Hearst arrived, Daly had organized the Anaconda Silver Mining Company, and had begun taking silver ore from the ledge. The results in silver and copper were not encouraging. At a depth of one hundred feet a seam of "copper-glance" was found. It was only a few inches wide, but it seemed to justify more extensive exploration. At two hundred feet a rich bed of copper was struck.

George Hearst made his usual examination, painstaking, unhurried and poised. He knew it was rich ore. He said to Daly: "It will make us a lot of money."

There were two and one-half feet of a copper ledge, besides the silver ledge three or four feet wide. The new mine was rich in both silver and copper. Hearst declared for deep development, and definitely settled on the most suitable place for sinking what is still the Anaconda shaft. In all mining history there has been no more accurate judgment.

Already Daly had let a contract for timber to build a mill. "Let us go a bit slow," said Hearst, who could be cautious even when opening up a bonanza. The contract was canceled, and a mill was leased instead. When the shaft was sunk at the place designated by Hearst, there were uncovered thirty feet of solid copper.

Hearst frankly admitted that he could not believe his

eyes. Still the shaft was sunk farther. Again Hearst could not believe his eyes. Copper was found from thirty to forty feet wide all the way down from two hundred to one thousand feet. "That was new business to us," Hearst said in writing of it. "No one knew much about that sort of thing."

The mining went on. The best ore was taken, but it was found that seven-eighths were left in the mine. It was discovered, also, that there was not enough silver to pay the very high freight. Both silver and copper must be had to make a profit. At that time copper was high, or the company would have made nothing. The next thing was to obtain water power. Hearst found water, bought land, and put in a race. He also started railroad works.

Hearst knew that in copper he was working blindly. He tried to employ a man from England or Germany who understood it. He heard of a man who had been foreman. Hearst employed him, and the young man began building an old-fashioned English furnace. At this time copper dropped to twelve cents so that no money could be made.

Hearst, Daly and Haggin dismissed their foreman and took charge themselves. They installed labor-saving machinery, and at last the Anaconda made money. Then copper had another fall. Hearst kept on buying claims and opening out. In 1889 the Anaconda had a big fire that did a million dollars worth of damage, and as he said "raised the devil generally." Then iron buildings were erected, that couldn't be burned.

In 1883 the Anaconda Company commenced the erection of a smelting plant at Warm Springs Creek, twenty-seven miles west of Butte. Later it became one of the largest copper smelting plants in the world.

The Anaconda sold, from 1881 to 1883 inclusive, thirty-three million, three hundred thousand pounds of ore. For the succeeding years of George Hearst's life the Anaconda copper production was:

| | | | |
|---|---|---|---|
| 1884 | 3,886,000 pounds | 1888 | 67,106,000 pounds |
| 1885 | 40,462,000 pounds | 1889 | 61,810,000 pounds |
| 1886 | 32,858,000 pounds | 1890 | 67,676,000 pounds |
| 1887 | 59,242,000 pounds | 1891 | 48,098,000 pounds |

In 1891 Montana took leading place as a copper producing state, and the Anaconda became the most celebrated copper mine on the American continent. George Hearst owned thirty shares, Haggin owned twenty-seven, Daly twenty-five, Terry seventeen. Hearst made a point of having five percent over a quarter.

The Anaconda was the largest and most easily worked mass of low grade ore in the world. The company owned a railroad, which delivered freight over thirty miles for eighty cents, and a fine hotel was built. Anaconda has a Hearst Free Library given by Phoebe Hearst. In Helena is a statue of George Hearst, who did so much to develop Montana.

In 1898 the Anaconda had spent seventy-two million in development. Every dollar was taken from the mine. It produced one-fifth of the world's annual copper supply, and employed five thousand men. The company owned ninety-one mining claims, and took out daily six thousand tons of ore. The veins varied from ten to one hundred feet. When Hamilton Smith, the great mining expert, recommended to the London Exploration Company the purchase of one-half of the Anaconda, he wrote that there was enough ore exposed for the mine to run fifty years. In 1899 the Anaconda produced one hundred and twenty-two million pounds of copper, besides several million dollars in gold and silver. Mrs. Phoebe Hearst sold her interest in the mine for several million.

# THE TWENTY-FOURTH CHAPTER

Hearst was essentially an American of the South and West. Back of him were Southern farmers, and far behind them were land owners of Scotland and England. Like most Americans with a background of the English yeoman, Hearst had in his blood little of the trader. He thought in terms of land. He was most at home, he breathed most freely, on a ranch. He liked to stand alone on a mountain top, or in a desert, and view wide spaces. He became one of the greatest land owners in California. When he died he had more than a million acres.

While Hearst was dealing in San Francisco real estate in the sixties, he made his most significant land purchase. In 1865 he bought for thirty thousand dollars the Piedra Blanca Ranch of forty thousand acres in the Santa Lucia Mountains jutting on San Simeon Bay near San Luis Obispo. He improved the little port of San Simeon for coastwise steamers, and in 1878 built a wharf. Hearst loved fine horses, and he had an ambition to breed cattle. His horses roamed the Piedra Blanca hills, and in the valley was his successful dairy ranch. He often took his friends to camp at San Simeon in the early days. Later he spent forty thousand dollars on buildings. He had a training track for his horses. The Piedra Blanca became one of the great stock farms of the state. This purchase was the nucleus of the San Simeon Ranch, which was later developed by William Randolph Hearst into one of the most beautiful showplaces in the world.

Hearst soon increased his acreage near San Simeon by buying the Santa Rosa Ranch, of three thousand acres, fifteen miles distant from the Piedra Blanca. Horses and cattle were moved back and forth between the two ranches.

The Piedra Blanca Ranch had an interesting history. In Spanish Piedra Blanca means white rock, for the rocks that look white off the coast of San Simeon. The first owner of the property was Don José de Jesus Pico, familiarly called Topoi Pico. He was the first cousin of Pio Pico, Mexican governor of California. Don Jesus led a stormy life. He was prominent in the Alvarado revolution, and for that service he was granted the Piedra Blanca in 1840. From 1841 to 1843 he was administrator of the San Miguel Mission. In 1846 he was "juez de paz" at San Luis Obispo. He supported Flores in the Natividad campaign against the Americans. He was captured, but paroled with other officers. In Salinas, Colonel John C. Frémont held an Indian servant of Don Jesus' and shot him as a spy. Then Don Jesus broke his parole, and was arrested by Frémont and condemned to death. Señora Picó, her fourteen children, and a number of San Luis Obispo Spanish-Californian women, threw themselves at the American commander's feet and begged for the life of Don Jesus. Frémont's own officers joined in the request. The American granted a pardon to Pico, and made a lifelong and useful friend.

Don Jesus helped to bring about the treaty of Cahuenga, which closed the Mexican War in California. His cousin, Don Andres Pico, after General Castro's flight, was in charge of the Spanish-Californian troops encamped at Los Verdugos, just north of Los Angeles. Don Jesus persuaded his cousin, Don Andres, that further resistance was useless. Immediately Don Andres reduced his command to less than one hundred men, made terms with the conqueror, and protected the lives and property of his soldiers.

After peace was declared, Don Jesus accompanied Fremont on his famous ride from Los Angeles to Monterey and back in 1847. Frémont wished to lay before General Kearny the probability of revolt threatened by Californians. Frémont and Don Jesus, accompanied by Jacob Dobson, left Los Angeles, March 22, 1847. They rode Californian mustangs, and drove nine unsaddled horses for frequent changes. The first night they slept at Captain Robbins' ranch near Santa Barbara. The second night they rested at San Luis Obispo. Here nine horses were changed for eight fresh ones of Pico's caballada. The third night they slept in the upper Salinas Valley, where they were frequently awakened by grizzlies. After conferring with General Kearny at Monterey, Frémont and Don Jesus returned to Los Angeles. They had ridden eight hundred miles in eight and one-half days, and were in the saddle one hundred hours.

After peace came between the Americans and Mexicans, Don Jesus lived on his Piedra Blanca Ranch, later bought by George Hearst. Don Jesus was the assessor of

San Luis County, and in 1852 and 1853 he served in the Assembly.

The San Simeon Ranch was originally a part of the church land of the Mission of San Luis Obispo. In 1842 it was granted by Governor Micheltorena to Don Jesus Ramon Estrada, of a famous Spanish-Californian family. The Santa Rosa Ranch was also in the beginning the property of the same Mission, but it was granted in 1841 to Don Julian Estrada, brother of Don Jesus Ramon's. A descendant of the Estradas, with his sombrero and silver embroidered saddle, was, for many years, the picturesque majordomo at the great San Simeon Ranch of William Randolph Hearst. He was Francisco Estrada, and was affiectionately called "Don Poncho."

In the eighties, George Hearst went over into Alameda County to look around for a little ranch where he could keep some horses. Near Pleasanton, in the hills, he found a cozy nest of five hundred acres. He did not develop the place, but later William Randolph Hearst built a hunting lodge there. When young Hearst bought the *New York Journal,* and went to live in New York, Mrs. Phoebe Hearst made additions to the hunting lodge, and under the supervision of Miss Julia Morgan, created the beautiful Hacienda del Pozo de Verona, where Mrs. Hearst lived and died.

George Hearst owned land in Tulare, Marin, Fresno and Butte Counties. He had timber land in Shasta and Siskiyou, and a large holding in Sacramento County. In the Feather River Canyon there is a station called Hearst, because George Hearst was one of the early investors in that region. He owned forty-five hundred acres in San Mateo County. In Texas he had a large acreage. He bought twenty-five thousand acres near Phoenix, Arizona. With Haggin and A. E. Head he purchased the Victorio cattle ranch in New Mexico. They had a quarter of a million acres, and controlled the water sources.

During the time of President Diaz, Hearst acquired six hundred thousand acres in southern Mexico. This property stretches through Vera Cruz, Campeche and Yucatan. Here are great forests of chicle trees, from which material for chewing gum is obtained. The rest is timber land and hardwood. At present there are no railway facilities, but in time the land will become very valuable. Hearst acquired this huge holding when he was mining in Durango. He found out that the Mexican government did not have a public land surveyor. Private individuals contracted for and surveyed land for the government. Hearst knew well the Mexican government officials, and he contracted to pay the expenses of surveying. For his work he received this land instead of money.

For years Hearst kept an observant eye on the vast Babicora Ranch in the State of Chihuahua, Mexico; but Geronimo and his Apaches were terrorizing that country. It was foolhardy to attempt improvements. The Babicora Ranch went begging during the Apache troubles. As soon as Geronimo was captured, in 1887, George Hearst closed for the Babicora at forty cents an acre. Shortly before his death the Mormons offered him a million for the property, but he would not sell. They wanted to found a colony. This Chihuahua ranch is two hundred and forty miles from the United States line. It is an enormous cattle range, and has been added to until now it has over nine hundred thousand acres.

Even before Hearst bought the Piedra Blanca Ranch he was greatly interested in fine horses. As early as 1864 he opened the Bayview track, famous in racing annals of San Francisco. This track was at Hunters' Point, near the old San Bruno Road, six miles from the heart of San Francisco. Hearst had a great affection for a young horse called King Thomas, the last of the King Ban strain. He would never tell what he paid for the animal at Tattersall's, but the price was said to be fifty thousand dollars, an enormous sum for that time. King Thomas was a disappointment to everyone but the owner, for he never developed real racing ability. Hearst did not murmur. When asked why King Thomas so greatly appealed to him, he answered with a quaint smile: "He is a friendly fellow. I like to rub his nose. He seems to know me."

Considerably later in life, after he became United States Senator, Hearst assembled a distinguished stable. Ballarat, Gorgo, Yosemite, and Tournament, were horses of celebrity. He talked to them as if they were children. Tournament was Hearst's most famous horse. He won the Realization and other great stakes. Ballarat was a sturdy Australian horse. On one occasion Ballarat was entered at Belmont Park. Pierre Lorillard had a horse in the race, and Charles Reed had a filly entered. Hearst, August Belmont, Lorillard and Reed were together. Suddenly Lorillard said: "Senator, I'll lay you one thousand my horse beats yours."

"Done," said the Senator.

"And I'll lay you another thousand my filly beats yours," answered Reed.

"Done," replied the Senator. Turning to his secretary, Andrew Lawrence, he asked: "Have we plenty of money?"

"Plenty," replied Lawrence.

"Bet another thousand on Ballarat to win in the pools."

The bet was made, and soon the horses got away. Belmont watched the race through glasses. He turned to the Senator and said: "You're going to win the race."

Ballarat was breezing along the stretch, when the Reed filly moved up on the inside. The jockey on Ballarat was Hayward, one of the best of his day. As the Reed filly came on, Hayward used his whip. Ballarat swerved and lost his stride for an instant. He quickly recovered, and the two horses came under the wire nose to nose, but the judges gave the race to Reed's filly.

Lorillard declared heatedly: "Senator, if that was my boy on my horse, I'd whip him."

"He did the best he could," was Hearst's only reply.

After the jockeys had weighed in, the Senator went to the paddock and, meeting Hayward, he said: "Well, my boy, you did the best you could."

"No sir, I didn't ride a good race. I went to sleep and let that filly crawl up on me. When I used the whip, Ballarat swerved."

"Didn't you know he always swerved if struck?"

"No sir." Tears came into the boy's eyes.

Senator Hearst gave him a friendly pat on the back and said: "You rode the best race you had in you."

Hearst decided that there was not proper cooperation between his trainer and riders, and so he substituted Cooper, the great colored trainer, for the man in charge. After that Ballarat and the stable were among the big winners of the year.

On another occasion the Senator had a horse called Yosemite in a race at Coney Island. The Hearst colors were almost identical with those of another stable. Yosemite won the race, but the judges placed him fifth, and gave the race to the horse carrying the colors similar to the Senator's. It was an astounding mistake. There was a great uproar, and a crowd surged around the Senator: "Are you going to permit that? Why don't you protest?"

The Senator stood, pulling his beard, and looking up at the judges in their stand. Then he said: "Judges are up there to decide. They made a mistake. Anybody's liable to do that."

Later the Association duplicated the purse, and Yosemite's share as a winner went to the Hearst stable.

Hearst raced for pleasant pastime, not profit, but sometimes his stable lost because of his betrayal by men he trusted. He never had reproaches for the delinquents, he merely changed his trainer, and kept on telling his jockeys how to ride; for none knew better than he. He had ridden bareback as a child. With his employees on the track, as elsewhere, he was always gentle and considerate. He rewarded loyalty with generosity, and a deaf ear for tale-bearing. When he found that his confidence had been imposed upon, he dismissed the incident with a good-natured quip or a homely saw. Probably he lost more than a million on his racing stable, but he did not protest. He never permitted defeats in pastimes to ruffle his serenity. He was a game sportsman.

## THE TWENTY-FIFTH CHAPTER

Hearst had a deep interest in politics, and his interest led him into the newspaper field. During a campaign when the purchase of a newspaper was suggested to him by some Democrats, Hearst replied: "I don't know any more about a newspaper than the man in the moon."

During the Garfield-Hancock campaign some of the Democratic leaders, Lloyd Tevis, Judge William T. Wallace, and Augustus Reis, said that the Democrats needed a newspaper. They were sure the party would subscribe toward starting one. Hearst answered: "Why do that? Why not buy the old *Evening Examiner*? There never has been any disgrace attached to the paper. It will serve our purpose." The Democratic leaders thought the suggestion brilliant.

Hearst looked over the business statements and accounts of *The Examiner*. He prided himself on being able to recognize a "salted mine," and this was the most dubious prospect he had ever seen. "Boys," said Hearst, "this looks like a quartz mill to me. It will take a great deal of money to put *The Examiner* on a paying basis."

"Don't worry. We'll all chip in," promised the Democratic boys. "We'll turn *The Examiner* into a morning paper. It will not cost more than ten or twelve thousand dollars. Buy the paper. We'll do our share."

Hearst bought *The Examiner*. Doubtless he smiled to himself when he entered journalism. He suspected who would be *The Examiner's* Santa Claus. And the Democratic leaders knew.

*The Examiner* was founded on the ruins of the *Democratic Press*, published by Captain William S. Moss. When the news of Lincoln's assassination reached San Francisco, the *Democratic Press* was wrecked by a mob. Captain Moss was charged with having Southern sympathies. He gave the *Democratic Press* a decent burial, but he started a new Democratic paper.

*The Examiner* was born as an evening paper on December 12, 1865. B. F. Washington, a grandnephew of George Washington, was editor. Moss, Philip A. Roach, and Charles L. Weller owned the paper for several years. Weller transferred his interest to George Pendleton Johnston. Moss, Roach and Johnston ran *The Examiner* for fifteen years. Jeremiah V. Coffey, afterward a revered Judge of the Superior Court of San Francisco, was chief editorial writer.

Of the three owners, George Pendleton Johnston was the strongest character. In 1855 he served one term in the Assembly, where he introduced and caused to pass an anti-dueling law. Three years later he was indicted and tried under the act he had fathered. One convivial evening Johnston was in the Bank Exchange Saloon on Montgomery Street, when State Senator William I. Ferguson of Sacramento spoke lightly of a lady. Johnston interposed. There were high words and drawn weapons, but no apology.

In those days an insult to a lady could be wiped out in Southern society only by a duel. Accompanied by their seconds the two men met with weapons, on lonely Angel Island. Three shots were fired without effect. Ferguson's second declared that honor was satisfied, but Johnston demanded an apology, or a continuation of the duel. Ferguson refused to apologize. The distance was shortened from ten paces to twenty feet. Johnston's bullet shattered Ferguson's thigh.

Ferguson lay on the ground dying. Johnston shook his hand. "Uncle Ferg," he said, "I'm sorry for you."

"That's all right," gasped Ferguson.

"That's enough said between gentlemen," replied Johnston.

Ferguson died. Johnston was tried and acquitted, but for twenty-six years he suffered under a terrible burden of remorse.

Shortly after he bought *The Examiner*, Hearst found that the Democratic leaders had no intention of meeting the paper's deficit. Their eyes took on a faraway look when it was even suggested. George Hearst never turned back. He was determined that *The Examiner*, like every other business undertaken by him, should be a success.

Hearst's son, William Randolph, was watching *The Examiner* venture with great interest from afar. He had been educated by tutors, and at the North Cosmopolitan Grammar School, the Lincoln Grammar School, and the Geary Street Grammar School. In 1881 he had entered St. Paul's School, Concord, New Hampshire, and later he went to Harvard, where he joined his friend Eugene Lent who was the business editor of the *Lampoon*, the

Harvard comic paper. Lent turned the position over to his friend, William Randolph Hearst, who placed the paper on a paying basis. This success was the foundation of William Randolph Hearst's future career.

George Hearst was losing several thousand a month in *The Examiner*. He was rapidly being taught that if it takes a quartz mine to run a quartz mine, it takes a paying quartz mine to run a losing newspaper. He set out to improve *The Examiner*. He let it be known that the paper was in the market for a new typographical dress. Immediately Palmer and Rey and Painter & Company, the leading type founders of San Francisco, sought his order. The two firms were asked to submit bids. The rival concerns cut each other's prices and got their figures down to bedrock. Hearst accepted the bid of Palmer and Rey. Painter & Company rushed to George Hearst to argue a forlorn hope. "I accept your bid," said Hearst.

"But Palmer and Rey—"

"I took their bid, too. A big paper like *The Examiner* needs two dresses. I can't buy cheaper; I accept both bids."

From 1880 to 1887 the maw of *The Examiner* was always open for more money. Hearst had no time to direct the paper, and he did not pretend to give it personal attention. He tried all sorts of people to make it a success. *The Examiner* came to be the leading Democratic newspaper of California, but it was always in "red ink."

William T. Baggett was publisher of *The Examiner*, and William T. Bogart was business manager. Major J. L. Tharp, afterward Commissary at San Quentin Prison, solicited advertisements. A business office was opened on the east side of Montgomery Street, near

Market, and there George Hearst appeared regularly to sign checks. He wore an amused smile, but he did not like a "red ink" newspaper any more than he liked a "red ink" mine. He was glad that the Ontario, the Homestake and the Anaconda were going strong.

*The Examiner* editorial rooms and the mechanical department were in an old building at 538 Sacramento Street. To the editorial rooms George Hearst seldom came. Here Clarence Greathouse was in charge. He was Hearst's lawyer and friend, a Kentuckian whose hobby was inventing a machine to milk cows with electricity. It was an idea that others were to perfect. Greathouse had no liking for journalism. Smoking innumerable cigarettes, he dictated editorials to his private secretary, George Palmer, who had arrived in San Francisco before the mast and was destined to have a long, brilliant career in the employ of William Randolph Hearst.

Greathouse never appeared at the office in the daytime. It was said that he feared to encounter reporters clamoring for larger salaries. Greathouse dared not drown the paper in "red ink." About eleven o'clock every night he appeared at the Wheeland and Collins' Place for a glass of port wine, after which he took the air for half an hour in a solitary ramble up and down deserted streets. There is a legend that a canny reporter one night lay in wait for him while he was sipping his port and extracted a two dollar raise.

Joseph M. Ward, a capable newspaperman, was city editor. He afterward wrote a novel, *Come With Me Into Babylon.* Other members of the staff were: John Coryland, telegraph editor; John Timmons, night editor; Paul Vandor, Felix J. Zeehandelaar, Andrew M. Lawrence,

Wallace F. Diss, James Donahue and Al (Blinker) Murphy. Jack Bryant was foreman of the composing room.

Editors and reporters were housed on the second floor of the building. Cubs were initiated as "space" and "detail" men. They were paid two dollars for the first detail, and one dollar for the second. They received twenty cents an inch for stories of their own discovery. Salaries for experienced men ranged from twenty to thirty dollars a week. City editor Ward received sixty dollars. These were not large salaries, but in those days money went a long way. There was an excellent "table d'hote" with a bottle of wine for fifty cents at the Frenchman's on Merchant Street, between Montgomery and Sansome. There was a German beer saloon on Montgomery Street where five cents bought a huge sandwich and a schooner of beer.

*The Examiner* had four pages, and went to press about half past three in the morning. The circulation was of very respectable size for those days, ten thousand copies. The paper exposed cruelty and graft at the House of Correction. There was an official investigation by the finance committee of the Board of Supervisors, with a jail break in the midst of it. *The Examiner* proved all its charges. Warden John Sedgwick, and a number of guards, were removed. One day during this excitement George Palmer drew two or three one-column cuts on chalk plates, and the next morning *The Examiner* readers were treated to the first illustrated news story ever published on the Pacific Coast.

George Hearst got considerable satisfaction out of the results of elections, even if *The Examiner* was in "red ink." It was generally conceded that but for the paper,

Garfield would have carried California. The Democrats all said: "Uncle George saved the state." Hancock carried California by ninety-four votes. Of the four Congressmen elected, two were Democrats. The paper supported Stoneman for Governor, and it helped George Hearst arrive in the United States Senate. Hearst secured the appointment of Greathouse as Consul General at Kanagawa, Japan. Greathouse was succeeded as managing editor by A. B. Henderson, a trained newspaperman who had made himself felt on the *Morning Call* as a formidable competitor.

Hearst liked *The Examiner*. He enjoyed reading it. It had only one fault, it devoured money. After the paper had lost about a quarter of a million, William Randolph Hearst left Harvard. Everyone called him Will Hearst. He had had a thoroughly good time in college. He had made himself known as an individual, and he had made a financial success of the *Lampoon*. George Hearst realized that his boy had not worked very hard as a student; he had had too much fun. He wondered what Will would like to do. He himself had spent large sums for lawyers. He thought Will ought to study law. He told his son so. He said he regretted that he hadn't studied law. So often he needed it in his business.

William Randolph Hearst had no interest in law as a career. He told his father he hoped that he would let him take *The Examiner*, and make a career of that. George Hearst was aghast at his son's choice. A newspaper wasn't a career—it was a deficit.

George Hearst took his boy to Mexico and showed him miles of land. There was money to be made in cattle on a large scale. Why not take charge of the Mexican property? William Randolph Hearst looked over the land and said he preferred the San Francisco *Examiner*. His father insisted that it was the worst choice he could make. He himself could not make *The Examiner* pay. How could a pleasure-loving youth, just out of Harvard, make a success of a newspaper that chewed up money as ravenously as the Anaconda Mine had in the beginning?

The tall, blond son from Harvard replied to his father, in his gentle, soft-voiced way: "Father, the reason you didn't make *The Examiner* pay was because it isn't the best paper in the country. I will make *The Examiner* the best paper in America."

"Take a look at the Ontario Mine, Will. Mining is a great career. The mines won't be worked out in America for a hundred years. There are mines in Mexico, South America, Africa. There will be fortunes in oil got out of California. I'll organize an oil company. Let's go over to Utah and look at the Ontario Mine."

William Randolph Hearst journeyed to Utah, and looked over the Ontario Mine. It was a great organization. He told his father so. No one more than he admired his father's mining genius, but firmly he came back to his first choice: "I'd like to have *The Examiner*."

George Hearst saw that his son had made up his mind. He agreed to stand by him for two years, and he made him a deed to *The Examiner* property. He did not think that his son would long endure the drudgery of turning a losing daily paper from "red ink" into "black." George Hearst was amazed when he discovered the capacity for work in the young college student, as amazed as when he found the great copper supply in the silver mine Anaconda. To his astonishment he saw his son, who had never known anything but luxury, enlarge *The Examiner* from four pages to eight, and settle down to be as hard a worker as his father ever was. George Hearst was delighted when he saw *The Examiner* circulation rise, and the advertising increase.

Before *The Examiner* was on a paying basis it cost its backer six or seven hundred thousand dollars, but at this time the paper was worth more than a million. George Hearst got much satisfaction out of reading the new *Examiner*. He said it had just as good eastern news as any other paper, and a great deal better western news. When he wanted all the news, he read *The Examiner*. In 1890 he said he did not think there was any better paper in the country. He was very proud of William Randolph Hearst, editor. In three years the boy had made good.

# THE TWENTY-SIXTH CHAPTER

WHEN George Hearst was twenty-six years old, he entered political life in Missouri. He went as a delegate to the state convention. Even in Nevada City he was deeply interested in politics. One of his friends who first knew Hearst when he was in his forties told the writer that had "Uncle George" studied law, as he would have liked, instead of following mining as a career, he undoubtedly would have been a statesman of high ability.

In 1865, for the second time, Hearst dabbled in politics when he went to the Assembly. Again in 1882, the love of politics was revived in him. An influential element in the Democratic Party persuaded him to allow his name to go before the state convention which was held in San Jose in the summer of 1882. At that time three beautiful rows of trees still shaded the wide Alameda, the Holy Way between Santa Clara and San Jose. An interesting group of men gathered in the "Garden City" for this convention. In the assembly hall was Denis Kearney, the sand lot agitator. Judge John Budd of Stockton was there, father of James Budd, a future governor of California. There was Judge David S. Terry, the fierce, fiery Texan, who had killed Senator Broderick in a duel, and soon was to fall victim to an ill-starred love and to the assassin's bullet. There was Stephen M. White, later to be United States Senator. Another delegate was George T. Marye, the last American to go as Ambassador to the court of the weak, tragic Russian Czar.

Hearst was placed in nomination for the governorship on June 21, 1882, by Judge Flournoy of San Francisco. "George Hearst," said Judge Flournoy, "is a type of the highest order of American manhood, developed by the spirit of our institutions . . . full of hope and ambition, rising from poverty in his youth. With good health, pluck and nerve, he came to California with those earlier characters who brought hither the genius of free government . . . He has been faithful and true. He is in his service to the Democracy of this state, the peer of any other man on this coast. In the honesty of his manhood he fears nothing . . . I hope his career may be an inspiration to the ambitious youth of this country. Common sense, genuine manhood, earnest labor, quickness of apprehension, decisiveness of purpose, independence of thought, adherence to his confidence in what is right, these make up the secret of his success . . . If he seeks now the opportunity to devote himself to the service of this state, it is because he knows in his heart of hearts that he will be faithful to his friends, true to the state where his labors have been blessed . . . Perhaps he did not have that early cultivation that so many men, more fortunate in their youth may have had, but he was richly endowed by nature with an honest purpose, with energy of character, with unflinching courage and with independence . . . Fortunate as he may have been in other respects, he is, above all things, fortunate in remaining simply George Hearst . . . There is no swerve in his nature . . . I believe that if he is selected, the doctrine of the new constitution and the laws of this state will be faithfully executed in Siskiyou, in San Francisco, in San Diego, and from the mountains to the sea."

Judge Niles Searls of Nevada City seconded the nomination, in a different vein. He spoke with the emotion of an old friend of the diggings. He told of Hearst's kindly deeds in the mines, of the innumerable benefactors that proved him incapable of forgetting an old friend. "In the pioneer days George Hearst came to Nevada County with small means, a pure heart, and an elegant backbone. He saved his money and amassed a fortune. He was no ordinary man. He was a prince clothed in the garb of a miner. If elected there will be no power behind the throne of George Hearst."

The picturesque past of the fifties lived again, and the convention was spellbound. Before Searls concluded his speech, George Hearst left the hall with tears in his eyes. "The old, old times," he said. "Searls makes me think of the days when I used the rocker, and of the boys that are dead and gone."

Before balloting began Hearst was presented to the convention and he spoke briefly: "If you expect a set speech of me, you will be sadly disappointed. I'm more of a worker than a man of words. [They cheered him.] I present myself before you for the nomination to the high office of Governor of the great state of California. I think I appreciate the responsibility of that high office. I think I understand the wants of the people of this state. [They cheered him again.] I endorse the platform adopted at the hands of this convention in every particular. [They cheered him more thunderously still.] If I receive the nomination I shall do whatever I can to make the administration thoroughly Democratic . . . That is, honest, pure, and in the interest of the people. But should this convention see fit in its wisdom to nominate any other gentleman, I shall be found in the ranks working for the ticket—the whole ticket—from top to bottom—just as though you had given me that nomination. [Again cheers.] I will not be a sorehead and whiner if I am beaten. I cast my lot with the Democratic party in my earliest manhood, and have done whatever I could to advance the interests of the Grand Old Party. I have lived on this coast for more than thirty years. I have been during all that time a hard worker, and I think I can modestly say that I did my share toward the development of the wealth and resources of my adopted state. [Still more cheering.] Whatever earnings I have made in mining operations on various parts of this coast I have invested in land and stock-raising, and necessarily had to employ a great number of men, all of whom have been white men, and not Chinese. At all events, all that I have, all that is near and dear to me, is in this state and I expect to remain here until I die and be wrapped in the clay of this Golden State. [They cheered him again.]

"Gentlemen, I believe that in the coming campaign we shall be successful, for I believe that the people of this state have finally concluded to take the management of the affairs of the government into their own hands. [Cheers again.] Gentlemen, I have no apology to make for myself. My living among these citizens for thirty-two years is the best evidence of what kind of man

I am. I am before you, and whatever I am you know. That is all I can say. Allow me to thank you."

There were several candidates, but the contest was between George Hearst and General George Stoneman. Fourteen ballots were taken before there was a choice. In the first seven ballots taken June 22, the leaders developed strength as follows:

Hearst—1,126; 2,128; 3,129; 4,134; 5,143; 6,146; 7,151.

Stoneman—1,117; 2,117; 3,123; 4,120; 5,122; 6,130; 7,136.

The following day Hearst maintained his lead over Stoneman up to the twelfth ballot; then the scattered votes began falling into the Stoneman column, while Hearst failed to gain. The result is told in these figures:

Hearst—8,159; 9,166; 10,169; 11,170; 12,174; 13,170; 14,170.

Stoneman—8,132; 9,133; 10,147; 11,166; 12,189; 13,204; 14,243.

The defeated candidate came upon the platform with the successful candidate, General George Stoneman. There was prolonged cheering. Stoneman said; "I made no promises. I beg pardon, I made one. I promised a friend of mine that if he ever got into San Quentin and I was Governor, I would pardon him."

Then George Hearst made what the correspondent of the San Francisco *Bulletin* described as the "best speech of the day." He said: "I had a pride to occupy the high office of Governor. I think that was an honorable pride, but I found in that contest a great general, a man who had defeated many armies, and it is not very astonishing that that gentleman defeated me. [Cheering drowned his words.] I thank this convention, and that little Spartan band that stood by me, from the bottom of my heart, and all I have to say to you is this: when I spoke to this convention the other day, I said I would not be a sorehead, and I'm going to keep my word. I am not going to squeal. Now, gentlemen, this is only the beginning of the fight, and if all you Democrats expect to win this fight easily, you're going to be greatly mistaken. You have placed a good man at the head of your ticket. Let me impress that upon you. True, I do not think it is necessary to impress it upon you, but I have to say something. [Laughter.] I want to be excused if I say something you all know, because I realize that the most ridiculous thing in the world is to try to teach a man something he has known all his life, and a man gets tired quicker than anything from hearing it. I mean to say, you have got something to do to win this fight. You have got the state patronage and the patronage of the general government against you, and I think you'll have to fight the corporations of this state. [A voice: "You bet your life."] I believe there will be more money spent against the General than all of us can raise. [Another voice: "I think so myself."] To beat money requires combination and union of action. Now, gentlemen, all I have to say, because I know you are tired, is that I will be found in the field as I told you, and will fight as bravely as if I had never been defeated. I'm not going to lose my generalship, either. [Cheers.]

"There are some others to speak here, and I will not detain you, though I could talk to you for an hour. I know some people have told you I could not make a speech. I know you have heard that I spelled bird with a u and which with a t, and that I cannot write more English than my name. That is all right now.

"You have also heard that I was worth ten million

dollars and twenty. I would like to be worth five million, but at the same time I do not propose that my money shall drive me out of the Democratic party. [How they cheered him!] But I want more so that I can spend more of it for Democracy without injuring myself and my family. After having said this I want you to understand that I'm not a sorehead, and if all the Democracy of the state will turn out and do what I will do, we will carry this state by fifteen thousand."

"If Uncle George had only made that speech before the balloting," remarked one of the delegates, "I guess he would not be a defeated candidate."

George Hearst only seemed a defeated candidate. No one is defeated who can go home after a repulse to a wife who is not cast down, but who is glowing with faith in her husband. Phoebe Hearst was at George Hearst's side in his ambition, always encouraging him, cheering him to greater effort and to ultimate victory. This was how she was when her husband returned from the San Jose convention. He thought for the moment that never again would he enter a political contest, but she knew better.

"Never mind," she said, "some day you'll go to the Senate."

# THE TWENTY-SEVENTH CHAPTER

EORGE HEARST kept his political promises. His money and his newspaper, *The Examiner*, were put wholeheartedly into the campaign of General George Stoneman, who had defeated him for the nomination. The Republicans nominated Morris Estee, but Stoneman was elected by a majority of twenty-three thousand and five hundred. The Legislature was overwhelmingly Republican. In 1885 when Governor Leland Stanford was elected to the United States Senate, George Hearst received the complimentary Democratic vote of thirty-seven to Stanford's seventy-nine.

One year later United States Senator John F. Miller, Senator Stanford's colleague, died in Washington, D. C. On March 8, 1886, while George Hearst was absent in Mexico on a business trip, Governor Stoneman appointed him to the vacant seat to serve until the California Legislature might elect Miller's successor.

Senator-elect Hearst's credentials were presented in the Senate on April 9, 1886, by Senator Leland Stanford, his colleague and old friend of Michigan Flat days.

George Hearst took the oath of office. Both California Senators came from the mining country, and both had been Sacramento merchants. Senator Hearst occupied the seat until July 3, 1886, when Abram P. Williams, a Republican, was elected to complete the unexpired term of General Miller.

During this first brief term in the Senate, Hearst was a member of the Committee on Railroads, the Committee on Manufactures, the Committee on Fisheries and the select committee to inquire into the claims of citizens of the United States against Nicaragua. All these were the late Senator Miller's assignments. Hearst was a hard working committeeman and he quickly understood the machinery of procedure. He rapidly gained friends for California, and acquired a reputation for fairness and understanding that made him very popular. His first speech was characteristic of him. It was in eulogy of his deceased predecessor, John F. Miller. Senator Miller was the president of the Alaska Fur Company. Shortly before his death he had been the subject of a ferocious attack by the Democratic Congressman, Barclay Henley, who charged him with corruption in administering the affairs of the Alaska Fur Company.

On May 27, 1886, the Senate gathered according to the time-honored custom to listen to the eulogies of the deceased colleague. Members of the Miller family were present, as were Mrs. Leland Stanford and Mrs. George Hearst. Phoebe Hearst was eager to hear her husband's first speech, and so were the members of the Senate. Eulogies were delivered by Senators Stanford, Fair, Edmunds, Harris, Logan and Voorhees. Then Senator Hearst was recognized and he spoke as follows:

"Mr. President: The Senators who have preceded me

have spoken of Senator Miller as a soldier and a states-man. It now becomes my privilege to speak of him as a citizen, in which capacity he also served his country.

"He and his associates were the recipients of one of the most important franchises in the gift of government. Out of this grew an enterprise which has been carried on to the best interests of all parties therein concerned. Their books have ever been open for the investigation of any authorized agent. In fact, to my knowledge, such investigation has always been invited.

"The management not only protected the government, but created a system which enabled the helpless and ignorant Indians engaged in work to save such a portion of their earnings that there is today to their credit in the banks of San Francisco, one hundred thousand dollars which might have gone into the coffers of the company for the simple consideration of five barrels of bad whis-key.

"This instance alone is sufficient to show the purity and integrity of the man's life. Such an example should be written on the mileposts of the highways, chiseled in the cliffs along the trails of the Rocky Mountains, graven on the granite of the Sierras, hewn on the tall pines of the Pacific Slope, and commemorated in the flowers in the valleys of the dead Senator's adopted state."

This outburst from the heart caused a commotion in the Senate, and earned for Senator the unqualified ad-miration of a body to which he was still a stranger. Pleased as he was with the praise received by him, he was proudest of all that his wife was present. He sensed her trembling anxiety when he opened his first speech. He felt her pride in him even before the applause came. When it ceased, he turned and said quietly to a friend, as he frequently did: "Miller was a good man. I know he was, because my wife says so. And my wife is always right."

From the beginning Senator Hearst took his position very seriously. He never spent any time in the cloak room. He was always at his desk. He said he didn't go to Washington to strut. He listened to everyone that cared to talk with him. He is supposed to have been responsible for the epigram that "The United States Senate is the best club in the world."

Hearst entered the Senate during the vogue of long-winded speeches. At times he was the only Senator listening to a speaker. He sat through his colleagues' speeches to the end, under the very nose of the speaker, not missing a word, nodding his appreciation, and manifesting a real interest. He was hungry for information. It is said to be a mark of genius to be so interested in life as never to be bored. One day the Senator sat for hours listening to a long speech composed mainly of statistics being delivered by the late Senator Hoar. Hearst's secretary asked him why he listened to dull and uninteresting speeches.

"I enjoy them," he replied. "Besides, I may want to make speeches myself."

Four days after Senator Hearst took his seat, he introduced his first bill, and by prophetic circumstance it was for the relief of the University of California. That bill marked the beginning of a long, distinguished connection of the Hearst family with the state university.

George Hearst knew the Pacific Coast with amazingly detailed accuracy. This was shown in the part he took in a debate during that first term on June 14, 1886. His store of knowledge confounded Senator Mitchell of Oregon, a friend of the Northern Pacific.

At that time there was a bill before the Senate proposing to restore to the United States the right to open for settlement lands granted to the Northern Pacific Railroad Company to aid in the construction of a railroad from Lake Superior to Puget Sound. The Northern Pacific was completed from St. Paul, Minnesota to Wallula, Washington, and from Portland to Tacoma on Puget Sound. Wallula is two hundred and fourteen miles east of Portland. The distance between Wallula and Tacoma across the Cascade Range is two hundred and sixty-two miles. Of this distance one hundred and eighty-seven miles were completed by the railroad, leaving seventy-five miles on top of the Cascade Mountains—of enormously difficult construction—still to be built. The Northern Pacific had failed to carry out the provisions of its conditional land grant.

It was proposed to forfeit the land adjacent to the seventy-five miles of uncompleted road on top of the Cascade Mountains, as well as the land from Wallula to Portland down the Columbia River. The Northern Pacific had not built a mile of the two hundred and fourteen mile stretch from Wallula to Portland, but it had a running arrangement with the Oregon Railway and Navigation Company between the two points. The land had been tied up for twenty-two years, with no prospect of a road being built. The producers in eastern Oregon, eastern Washington Territory, and Idaho Territory, in their efforts to transport their freight to seaboard, did not care to continue at the mercy of a railroad and a line of steamers on the Columbia River under single control.

Senator Hearst on this occasion showed his interest in

the producers of this faraway region. This was disclosed in his questioning of Senator Mitchell. Hearst's cross-examination revealed a keen intellect. His part in the debate was as follows:

Mr. Hearst: "Will the Senator from Oregon allow me to ask him a question? — I understand that the road for which the Senator from Oregon wishes to retain the land, is a road from Wallula to Puget Sound. — What benefit will that be to Portland? — I do not know just how far the Northern Pacific Railroad goes down to the Columbia River. — I understand Wallula to be near Walla Walla. — In other words, the proposed road connects with the Northern Pacific there and goes to Puget Sound across the Cascade Mountains? — I understand the Columbia River runs to Puget Sound, but the road has no connection with its own line from where it strikes the river until it gets to Wallula. Is that the fact? — In going from Portland I went down the river and took a railroad that went to Puget Sound, which I understand is the Northern Pacific. — The Northern Pacific has no connection from there to Wallula with its own road from Portland? — It seems a matter of very great importance to have the road finished down the river to connect with the road to Puget Sound. — That is very unfortunate. — Would not the Senator be willing to give them that land provided they would build down the river? — If the Senator from Oregon will yield to me, I wish to ask him a question. I am no lawyer, and may not be familiar with the principles to be applied in this case, but I should be very loath to vote for any bill to forfeit the land from Wallula to Portland, for the reason that the company has all the good land now. If we could compel them to finish the road from Wallula to Portland

and give them bad land, it certainly would be a good trade for the United States, and particularly for Portland, Oregon. Therefore I should be very loath to change any condition of the grant if the company could be compelled in any way to complete the road. If they have built part of the road and got all the good land, it seems to me there ought to be some way to make them build the rest of the road and take the bad land. — It is a broad grant, but, in traveling along the Cascades as far as any one can see down the river it is miserably poor. — Does not the Senator think that the people of Oregon would be very glad to give that land up if they could get competition from Wallula to Portland and connect with the Northern city down the river? — Why is it that you go in and invite them to have the land across the Cascade Mountains, to give them in connection to Puget Sound, when you leave out all the Willamette Valley and the trade which naturally comes to Portland? — You have a competing line from Wallula to Puget Sound from the east. — I think from the questions asked that the Senators on this side of the Chambers understand it. — It has been a long time since I was there, and there was no railroad built along the river then. I have only obtained my knowledge from the papers, and I have not read much about the matter for a year or two. I understand the Senator to say that at Puget Sound you can get on the cars and go to Portland by the Northern Pacific. — Then I understand that you have connection from Portland up the river on the Northern Pacific. — Then why have you not a complete line? — So the Northern Pacific has not built the line? — That is the way I thought it was. — You get nothing except you make an arrangement by a single line from Portland to Wallula? The Northern

Pacific has no connection? — The only advantage the people get by competition is the continuance of this line from Wallula across the Cascades to the Sound? — That to Portland is out of the way. — Then Senators may understand that after this line gets to this Sound the Northern Pacific will have a road that runs across the country south and east, until it strikes the Sound and thence to Portland? — So by going eighty or one hundred miles out of the way the people could get an opposition line?"

In the River and Harbor Appropriation Bill, Senator Hearst discovered a loosely drawn phrase, designed to prevent the hydraulic mining in California, but actually endangering the entire mining industry. Hydraulic mining was under the ban of a Federal Court injunction, and the provision in the River and Harbor Bill was unnecessary. Senator Hearst saw grave danger in this language: " . . . hydraulic mining by water through pipes and used through nozzles under pressure . . . "

During the debate on the general measure, Senator Hearst called attention to this phrase and offered an amendment, saying:

"We want to prevent these things going into the channels, and if we stop hydraulic mining, we stop this business. These people have been so industrious that they have made inventions by which they can lift up and wash out a ton of stuff by a force of water five miles away for five cents. The consequence is that these great inventions have disarranged things so that they have changed the face of nature to some extent. There is one kind of mining that interferes with the stream. We want to be very careful in discarding it so as not to interfere with people who occupy a country four hundred miles

long and forty miles wide and who produce out of that little belt of country about twenty million annually, which you people in the East need very badly to pay your balances. I want to offer one amendment so as to define what hydraulic mining is. For my own part, I do not think the provision ought to be in this bill at all, because the thing had been litigated thoroughly, and everyone of the people is under perpetual injunction from the United States Circuit Court today against doing what is complained of."

Senator Hearst then offered an amendment inserting after the word "pressure" the words "and against mountain sides or natural banks," so that the passage read: " . . . hydraulic mining by water through pipes and used through nozzles under pressure and against mountain sides or natural banks."

"I think," said Senator Hearst, "that my colleague will agree with me. I do not think that my colleague or any one from any part of the world has any objection to any kind of mining in California except hydraulic mining. I have endeavored to get the bill framed both in committee and here so as to stop that. I think that two-thirds of all the people in California are willing to do that. Of course, it is a hardship, because we stop the investment of millions of dollars doing that; but we ought not to go further. I have my pocket full of letters and telegrams coming every day expressing fears that by this action the whole mining industry in the Sierra Nevadas will be destroyed."

The amendment was adopted. George Hearst had the satisfaction of knowing that his old friends in the Sierra Nevadas were breathing freely again.

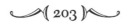

# THE TWENTY-EIGHTH CHAPTER

WHEN Grover Cleveland was President, his administration, in making appointments, frequently ignored the recommendations of Senators and Representatives. During Senator Hearst's short term he found that the President preferred to select his own officials rather than take counsel with the new California Senator. The result of this independence on the part of the President was that Senator Hearst became equally independent. He remained away from the White House. Doubtless President Cleveland was surprised to find the new Senator as free from subserviency as himself.

Andrew Lawrence, correspondent of the San Francisco *Examiner*, was summoned to the White House by Daniel Lamont, secretary to the President. After Lawrence had been introduced by Secretary Lamont, President Cleveland asked: "Why doesn't Senator Hearst come to see me?"

Lawrence replied: "That is as much your fault as his, Mr. President."

There was an awkward pause, then the President said:

"Will you tell Senator Hearst for me that I wish he would call on me?"

The next morning Lawrence conveyed the message to the Senator. Hearst had the habit of pulling at his beard when he was thinking hard. "Well, if the President wants to see me, I suppose I will have to go, but I don't think he has treated our friends right."

"Tell him so," urged Lawrence.

"I don't want to quarrel with the President," was the characteristic reply.

Senator Hearst went to the White House at five o'clock that evening. Lamont afterward wrote Lawrence that President Cleveland said that he had never met a more friendly, winning personality than Hearst's. This interview marked a change in the Cleveland administration. From that time Senator Hearst was consulted on all appointments, not only in California, but up and down the Pacific Coast.

It was fortunate that complete harmony prevailed between President Cleveland and Senator Hearst because the new Senator exercised much influence with the President during the so-called "Cutting Incident" of 1886. A. K. Cutting, American editor of a newspaper at Paso del Norte in the State of Chihuahua, Mexico, called Emigdio Medina, a rival editor, among other things, "a fraud." From this editorial outburst, trivial as it was, developed a situation that threatened to embroil Mexico and the United States in war.

At the instance of Medina, Cutting was arrested. To avoid punishment, he went through the form of reconciliation and was released. Then Cutting crossed to El Paso and inserted a card in the El Paso *Herald*, reiterating that Medina was a fraud and adding that he was a dead-

beat and a contemptible coward. On his return to Paso del Norte, Cutting was arrested and lodged in jail. This was the first of July, 1886.

The American Consul at Paso del Norte demanded Cutting's release, but he was ignored. The Consul-General at the City of Mexico fared no better. The American Ambassador to Mexico found Mexican officialdom polite but firm. Meanwhile, the State Department at Washington had been appealed to. American newspapers fanned the angry flames. The fact that Cutting was jailed in Mexico for an offense committed in the United States, especially irritated Americans. Behind the illegal punishment of an obscure individual, American editors saw a deliberate effort to infuriate and humiliate the "gringo" above the Rio Grande. American editors were on the warpath. President Cleveland backed them up.

Cutting was still in jail, and the newspapers daily grew more hysterical. Then Consul Brigham, at Paso del Norte, sent this wire to Secretary of State Bayard, on July 22, 1886: "Mexico massing troops at this point; one hundred and fifty men this morning, and two thousand said to be on the way. Cutting still in prison. Great excitement."

At this point Senator Hearst took a hand. He and President Cleveland were friends. He knew and admired President Porfirio Diaz. He understood and was sympathetic with the mind of Mexico. So he went to President Cleveland, counseling moderation, giving excellent reasons for his advice. He spoke from firsthand knowledge of Mexico and Mexican character.

Hearst's advice so prevailed that when, a few days later, the President sent a message to Congress, it proved to be merely the routine transmission of a letter from

Secretary Bayard. The Secretary declared: "The present case may constitute a precedent fraught with the most serious results." President Cleveland himself was silent. This was so unexpected that Congress calmed, and the newspapers cooled down.

The Governor of Chihuahua ordered the local authorities to bring Cutting to trial immediately. He was convicted and sentenced to a year's imprisonment at hard labor, and the payment of a fine, and of an indemnity to Emigdio Medina. But the Mexican Supreme Court, while skillfully evading the international legal points involved, promptly exonerated Cutting from all penalties, and set him free. After these two gestures, the Mexican crisis passed, and at the close of this session of Congress Senator Hearst retired to private life.

# THE TWENTY-NINTH CHAPTER

I̶N the following November Washington Bartlett, a Democrat, was elected Governor of California. A Democratic Legislature was also chosen, and in January 1887, George Hearst was returned to the United States Senate. He took his seat in that body on March 4, 1887. On that same day the San Francisco *Examiner* became the property of his son, William Randolph Hearst, and a new era in American journalism began.

Senator Hearst returned to Washington to serve a six year term, but he faced the handicap of belonging to the minority party. Grover Cleveland was President. The Republicans were in control of both branches of Congress. All that the Senator could accomplish was by shrewd common sense, plain dealing and a pleasing personality that insured popularity. He became the personal friend of every member of the Senate, Republican and Democrat alike. Among those whose term of service began with his were William M. Stewart of Nevada, Matthew S. Quay of Pennsylvania, Eugene Hale of

Maine, Cushman K. Davis of Minnesota, John W. Daniel of Virginia and William E. Chandler of New Hampshire.

Hearst was one of the richest men in the Senate, and soon there was no more attractive house in Washington than the residence created by Mrs. Hearst on New Hampshire Avenue. She rebuilt a large dwelling, and added an art gallery. The walls were hung with silk, and the house was filled with rare paintings, tapestries and objects of art collected by her during her many trips to Europe. A firm of Baltimore decorators rearranged and decorated the house. Senator and Mrs. Hearst were proud that the work was American.

Before Mrs. Hearst went to Washington she had become not only a beloved hostess in San Francisco, one who always remembered faces and names, and had worthwhile and distinguished people for her guests to meet, but she educated boys and girls privately and gave large sums to charity. She helped Sarah B. Cooper establish a free kindergarten, and she aided the first college settlement in San Francisco in 1883. She gave generous support to the Hahnemann Hospital, the Infant Shelter, the Old People's Home, the Homeopathic Hospital, and the Children's Hospital.

In Washington her benevolence had a new and wider field. She helped the Free Kindergarten and the Cathedral School. She rescued Mount Vernon from ruin, and restored the original furniture. To her New Hampshire Avenue residence came a stream of celebrated people from all over the world, but Senator Hearst did not care much for celebrities, unless they had a western background. He never wore evening dress, but he compromised occasionally by wearing a frock coat of broadcloth. Frequently he found a western crony among the guests, and dragged him off to a hidden spot to have a real chat. Often he was found with Colonel Tom Ochiltree, Arthur McEwen, or Mark Twain. He preferred being called "Uncle George" to Senator. He liked his old friends of the mining camps, just as he liked the old-time foods of the camps. He dined on gold plate, but the Hearst chef knew that the Senator must have pork spareribs and hominy, or string beans with two strips of bacon.

A story is related by Mrs. Philip King Brown, who as Miss Nellie Hillyer, often visited the Hearsts. They had run over from Washington to New York, and were stopping at the Hotel Brunswick. During the dinner hour a bellboy brought a plain white card on which was written: "It is now proposed further to discuss the robbery."

The card was unsigned. Senator Hearst laughed. "That's Mark Twain. It's his way of talking about the publishing business he wants me to back." Then he turned to the boy and said: "Show him up."

Miss Hillyer, with keen interest for collecting, realized that the card had a value, and she asked Senator Hearst to give it to her. When Mark Twain appeared in the Hearsts' room, Miss Hillyer asked him to sign the card. This he did in the words: "Success to Crime! Mark Twain." The Senator backed the publishing house of Mark Twain, but it ended in bankruptcy.

Senator Hearst always found at his wife's receptions a stream of men eager to hear him talk, to listen to his experiences, and to ask his judgment. He enjoyed his wife's parties, but he often protested against going to other people's entertainments. In the end he always succumbed to Mrs. Hearst's persuasion by saying: "Puss, if you want me to go, I'll go."

Best of all he enjoyed the evenings when he was alone with his wife and a few relations or old friends. Then he used to say: "Puss, get out the begging letters. Let's read them."

There was always a large box of these letters from all over the United States. Money came to Hearst like a river, and he let it flow from him like a river. Mrs. Hearst gave lavishly, but when she read some of the letters from parasites and people that she knew to be incurably undesirable she protested against making further gifts. The Senator always said: "Let's give all of them something." When he had spent an evening answering dozens of letters, making dozens of people happy with checks, he considered he had attended a pleasant party.

The Hearsts were not long in Washington before they held an unique place in the life of the city. The wife of the President is not supposed to return visits, but lovely young Mrs. Cleveland frequently spent a morning with Mrs. Hearst. This friendship continued throughout Mrs. Hearst's life. Mrs. Cleveland later brought her second husband, Professor Thomas Preston, to the Hacienda, near Pleasanton, when she came to California.

Mrs. Hearst kept pace with her husband's generosity. When she crossed the continent she never forgot to have gifts for the fireman and engineer. Once while snowbound for nine days she supplied food for everyone on the train. In those days before "ready-to-wear" clothing, she bought for the wives of her workmen yardage, buttons, thread, hooks and eyes, complete dresses by the dozen. She had a fireproof storehouse for her gifts. Christmas was one of the happy times of her life. No sooner was one Christmas over, than she began making ready for the next Christmas. Many a gentlewoman in reduced circumstances lived for years by making Christmas gifts for Mrs. Hearst, who always paid the most generous price for everything. One of Mrs. Hearst's protégées said to the writer: "The Hearsts were the biggest and best experience in the lives of everyone they met."

# THE THIRTIETH CHAPTER

D URING the last years of his life, George Hearst lived in Washington, but San Francisco and California had his deepest affection. He fought for California in the Senate, and never tired of singing her praises. "The day will come," he used to say, "when we shall regret drawing people to California. We'll want to build a Chinese wall along the Sierra Nevadas to keep out newcomers and preserve the most wonderful state in the Union for ourselves."

Hearst was indefatigably active in obtaining badly needed public buildings for California. When he introduced his bill for a public building in San Diego, Senator Hoar, a giant of influence, objected, and Hearst replied:

"Mr. President, I am sorry that any one objects to this bill. No doubt it appears a little strange to some to see Senators standing up here and claiming something for California. I desire to inform the Senate that my state has been neglected in the past, perhaps more on account of the neglect of our representatives in making known our wants than from any intention on the part of the general government to do us an injustice.

"I say this because in my conversation with the representatives from the various states in this nation I find a disposition on their part to grant us anything we may ask within reason. This is not strange, for our state is made up of people from every state and territory in this Union, and is destined to be the health-pleasure-seeking resort of America.

"Mr. President, we have been a state for nearly forty years, and we have only one post office building, and that is in San Francisco. It has to be propped up to keep it from falling. It is built on piles near the water front, is entirely outside the center of population, totally unfit and wholly inadequate to the wants of our present population, which is now about four hundred thousand.

"Mr. President, I feel that it is a disgrace to the government, and to the city of San Francisco, where I have the honor to reside. You can pardon me for feeling thus, when you call to mind the fact that California has contributed to the national treasury from its various sources of revenue from twelve to fourteen million dollars annually during our existence as a state. We have done more than all this. We have dug out of the earth, by our energy and enterprise, twelve hundred million of gold, thereby creating that much additional wealth that went into the circulation as money, increasing property values from one hundred to three hundred percent. We also enabled the government to pay its balances in gold by furnishing them forty or fifty million a year at the time when it was most needed.

"Mr. President, I am very glad indeed to know that so many distinguished Senators have visited my state

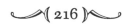

within the last year, which in part accounts for their friendly assistance to this bill. All the Senators who have spoken have visited California within the past year, except the distinguished Senator from Wisconsin, Senator Spooner. He is a member of the Committee on Public Buildings and Grounds, and is well informed on this bill, as he is upon all subjects he discusses in the Senate.

"I traveled with these distinguished Senators all over my state. We rode together on the beautiful Bay of San Diego, and were thus afforded an opportunity of seeing its magnificent harbor, also the beautiful and growing city of San Diego with its population of thirty thousand. I found upon examination that the postal receipts of San Diego, within the last ten years, had grown from practically nothing to the handsome sum of sixty thousand annually, the customs receipts reaching up into hundreds of thousands yearly, and the population steadily increasing. It is also rapidly becoming a great railroad center.

"Mr. President, the Senate will remember that there are but two harbors where ships can be safely loaded in bad weather in central and lower California, San Francisco and San Diego; San Francisco being five or six hundred miles north. Of course, you can unload ships along the coast in many places, if the weather is pleasant, and the water calm. This beautiful harbor from which at least five hundred thousand people get their coal and supplies—"

Mr. Morgan: "Where does this coal come from?"

Mr. Hearst: "From Australia, and is landed there in great quantities. It is on the border near Mexico and it therefore becomes important as a military post.

"Mr. President, we ask only the modest sum of three hundred thousand dollars to purchase a site and erect a

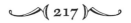

building for a post office, custom house, and other public uses for a city destined to become one of the largest cities on the Pacific Coast.

"Mr. President, the Senator from Alabama [Mr. Pugh] said the other day that he was the silent man of the Senate. Sir, I am the silent man, and I do not intend that he shall take my place. [Laughter.] While I am up I want to say that we intend to present claims to the Senate for public buildings at this session and to present them for cities all over my state that are justly entitled to them. We intend to do it honestly. We do not intend to ask for three hundred thousand and expect but one hundred thousand. We expect to get every dollar we ask for. We will show in every case that we are entitled to it.

"We shall prove the amount asked for in every instance is not exorbitant by every Senator who honored our state by his presence, and thank goodness there are a goodly number, among whom are several of the oldest and ablest men in this body.

"Mr. President, I shall ask for a post office building for San Francisco, to take the place of the dilapidated old rookery we have there now. I expect a good one, and I want a large sum of money for it.

"I shall ask one for the beautiful city of San Jose, called the 'Garden City' situated in the heart of the magnificent Santa Clara Valley.

"I have asked you to increase the appropriation heretofore made for Los Angeles, the metropolis of southern California, a city we are all proud of.

"I have asked that a public building be given to the city of Oakland, the 'Brooklyn of California.'

"I have asked an increase in the appropriation for a public building in Sacramento, the capital of our state, a railroad center, situated in the heart of the Sacramento Valley.

"I have asked that Stockton, situated in the midst of as fine an agricultural country as you will find in the world, be given a public building.

"I ask that these appropriations be made because of the importance of these cities, and because their receipts to the government and their rapidly increasing business and population justly entitle them to it. We have other cities that may claim your attention hereafter."

Mr. Mitchell: "If the Senator from California will allow me to interrupt him—"

Mr. Hearst: "Certainly."

Mr. Mitchell: "I can vouch for everything he says in relation to the San Francisco post office. I think that post office is a disgrace to the city."

Mr. Hearst: "I thank the Senator from Oregon for his interruption and for his very truthful remarks; everybody who has seen it will agree with us."

The Vice-president: "The Senator's time has expired."

Mr. Sherman: "I hope the Senator from California will be allowed to proceed by unanimous consent."

The Vice-president: "Is there objection? The Chair hears none, and the Senator from California has unanimous consent to proceed."

Mr. Hearst: "Never mind. Let us pass the bill. I shall have ample opportunity to speak on other appropriations that I shall ask for California."

Senator Hoar gravely announced: "The junior Senator for California has given me the information I desire, and I shall vote aye." San Diego obtained its appropriation.

During the debate on the question of land grants in New Mexico and Arizona, Senator Stewart criticized the land policy of Mexico as it affected Americans. Senator Hearst knew Mexico, and liked its people. He had become an intimate friend of president Porfirio Diaz. He had invested heavily in Mexican land and in Mexican mines. He sprang to the defense of Mexico, at the same time expressing his opinion on the subject under debate:

"Will the Senator [Stewart] permit me to ask him a question? Do you know of one single case ever presented to the Republic of Mexico which was not sustained by the Mexican Government? I speak of land on which citizens lived. — They were conditional grants and grants of this kind: A kind of go-between fellow would get a lot of land for the purpose of making settlement and would get hold of it and not build a house or get anybody to live there. The government did better than our government has done. It settled the question, and said if in a certain time a house was not built and cattle were not on the ranch, that was the end of it. Now, what we need in this case is something that will make an end of it sometime or other.

"While I am up I will say that I think this four million grant serves a very good purpose here about every five minutes. I doubt myself whether there is any such grant in Arizona or New Mexico, but it answers the purpose here to make out that the whole country is covered with grants and that they are all genuine.

"My opinion is that three-fourths of all the claims in New Mexico and Arizona are fraudulent, and so it will all be decided when the court gets there. That is what the honest people there want. There were hundreds of claims taken up twenty-five or thirty years ago by stockmen, and they have run themselves into Spanish grants according to their notion. It may be that they have a

Spanish writing to show something about it. So it goes all over the country. But there are genuine, good people living there, Germans who were transferred from Mexico to this country, and some Americans who were transferred, and many good old Spaniards. If you go there, they will give you a horse and saddle to ride around, and you can stay a month, and they will never charge you a cent. They have no law to protect them from anyone going into their peach orchard and making a settlement there today. They cannot go before a constable or justice of peace, and they have been living for thirty years under a government that agreed to protect them."

Hearst's principal committees were Indian Affairs, Mines and Mining and Pacific Railway Commission. He took committee work seriously, but rarely spoke on the floor of the Senate.

"I believe it is a mistake," he said, "to speak too much in the Senate unless you want to get something for the people at large." When he did speak, he commanded attention.

When Congress considered the admission to statehood of Washington Territory, an attempt was made to incorporate part of Idaho Territory in the new state. Senator Stewart of Nevada was willing to carve out a part of Idaho for Washington in order that Nevada might absorb the remainder. He assumed that his lifelong friend, George Hearst, would support him. To his consternation, Hearst flatly opposed him. Stewart indignantly stroked his beard when Hearst spoke as follows:

"Will the Senator allow me to ask him a question? Are you perfectly familiar with the valleys of Idaho? — Does the Senator not know that around Lewiston is one of the finest agricultural countries in the United States? —

Leaving there and going up Snake River there is fine land. When you get through the canyon, there is a valley about six hundred miles long and forty miles wide that would hold two or three million people. It has the finest land in all the world. There are many valleys running up into the mountains which are fine agricultural lands. Eastern Idaho does not need irrigation as the Senator well knows.

"There is very little waste land in Idaho. I should like the Senator to tell me where there is much waste land in Idaho. It abounds in rivers with large rich valleys, and the tops of the mountains are covered with the finest kind of timber. Take, for instance, the Owyhee River with a valley twenty-five miles long and six or eight miles wide, and Breneau River putting into Snake River, with a valley twenty miles long and five or six miles wide. The territory abounds in rivers such as Snake River, Clearwater, Belouse, Pen d'Oreille, Kootenai.

"At the lower end of these rivers the hills and valleys are rich, and at the heads of the valleys there is the finest timber possible. The mountains are terrible mountains, but there is not better country for mining that I know of in the United States. That is the very roughest portion of Idaho. I think it would make one of the grandest states in the Union.

"Certainly, there is very little waste land there. — But that is not the eastern portion. The eastern portion does not have to be irrigated; it is only the interior valleys. The Senator will admit that it is one of the best watered regions in the United States. — That may be so, but Jack Gilmore staged over that country for ten years. He tells me that the Snake River Valley above the falls will support two million people. Where that land is not rich, it abounds in the best kinds of timber. It is the best timbered portion of the United States. — If the Senator will allow me, I will state that I have been all over the territories west of the Rocky Mountains as much, perhaps, as any other man, and I think Idaho has more agricultural land in it than all the other territories."

That speech destroyed forever the schemes of Washington and Nevada. It saved Idaho for statehood.

"George," said Stewart, when Hearst had finished speaking, "I thought you were with me."

"With you on almost anything, Bill," was the reply, "but this time I don't think you're right."

In the same straightforward fashion he took a stand against his colleague, Stanford, when he introduced the Central Pacific Railroad Bill. He did not think Stanford was right.

Hearst opposed the bill against oleomargarine, although he himself had a large stock ranch at San Simeon. He explained his opposition in this way: "I smoke dollar cigars, the best I can buy, but I can smoke old pipes in the mines. If people can't afford to buy my butter, let them have oleomargarine."

THIS BUILDING STANDS
AS MEMORIAL TO
GEORGE HEARST
A PLAIN HONEST MAN
AND GOOD MINER

# THE THIRTY-FIRST CHAPTER

U NTIL the final days of his life Hearst enjoyed and was interested in his work in the Senate. He became greatly disturbed by the possibility that the Force Bill before Congress in 1890 might become a law. This, the third and last, Force Bill of American history, aroused deep enmities. Senator Hearst held it a measure of undiluted iniquity. Introduced in the House of Representatives by Congressman Henry Cabot Lodge, it proposed to amend the election laws of the United States by giving the Federal supervisors of elections and special deputy marshals a coercive authority never before possessed by them. It also empowered the Federal Government to use troops at the polls. After a fierce struggle the Force Bill passed the House July 2, 1890. Then it was heatedly and bitterly debated in the Senate. Senator Hearst was foremost in the battle. He never spared himself. All his life he defied hardships and throve on labor that broke the endurance of other men. His work was his pastime. He ignored the fact that he was seventy. He saw his friends drop around him, but he lived as if death would pass him by, and even his flesh would be immortal. To the last his head was erect, and his shoulders squared.

Then disease struck. Hearst's health broke, his body crumpled. The pioneer had reached the end of the trail.

In December 1890, Senator Hearst went to New York to consult his physician, Dr. Charles Ward. The medical man confirmed the Senator's own intuition about the gravity of his illness. Hearst hastily returned to Washington to join his wife and his son, William Randolph Hearst, who came from San Francisco to be with his father for the last time. The-Man-That-Earth-Talked-To went on gallantly. In the inevitable aloneness of nearing death his life was a daily torture, but he showed great courage, and spoke no word of complaint. In spite of his illness he inquired often as to the fate of the Force Bill. He wished to see it defeated before he himself passed from life. His wish was fulfilled. By a coalition of the Republicans and Democrats, the Force Bill was killed on January 5, 1891.

Quite calmly Hearst often spoke of death. "I'm not afraid to die," he said to Dr. Ward. "It is the lot of man. I only regret leaving my family and the good friends who have been with me."

Dr. Ward replied: "Senator, you have said goodbye to your friends many times without regret, for you knew you were coming back. Now when you say goodbye the last time it will be their regret."

George Hearst was instinctively religious, though he was not a constant church-goer. Sometime before his death he said: "I believe that the great Being who made me has some place prepared for me; but how, or where, I do not know. I see no reason why we should not exist hereafter as well as here. There is as much reason for a future world as for our present one. I believe in the moral lessons derived from religion, and I have the highest reverence for Christ."

In that faith he died. So quiet and peaceful was his leave-taking that his wife and son, who were holding his hands, did not know he had gone. He ceased to breathe at ten minutes after nine o'clock Sunday evening, February 28, 1891.

The Senate was in the turmoil of an all-night session when Senator Stanford arose shortly after midnight and announced that his colleague from California had passed on. The Senate at once adjourned as a mark of respect. Immediately afterward the news was given to the House of Representatives by Thomas J. Clunie of California.

The body lay in state at the Hearst residence, 1400 New Hampshire Avenue, until Thursday, March 5. Then brief and simple religious obsequies were performed by the Reverend Doctor Douglass of Saint John's Episcopal Church. The group of mourners included President and Mrs. Benjamin Harrison, and Vice-president and Mrs. Levi P. Morton. Then the casket was placed aboard the funeral train of six Pullman sleepers and day coaches. In addition to Mrs. Hearst, William Randolph Hearst and a few intimate friends, the train carried eight United States Senators and nine members of the House who had been named as escort of honor. They were Senators James L. Pugh of Alabama, Francis B. Stockbridge of Michigan, Zebulon B. Vance of North Carolina, Charles J. Faulkner of West Virginia, William B. Bate of Tennessee, James H. Berry of Arkansas, John S. Barbour of Virginia, Philetus Sawyer of Wisconsin; and Representatives Thomas J. Clunie of California, L. E. McComas of Maryland, Seth L. Milliken of Maine, Thomas J. Geary of California, James S. Sherman of New York, H. St. G. Tucker of Virginia, Charles H. Gibson of Maryland, Joseph E. Washington of Tennessee and T. C. Catchings of Mississippi.

The mourning train moved out of Washington toward the setting sun. For the last time George Hearst was going West. Across Ohio, Indiana, Illinois, he came to the Mississippi. Did he remember its wide waters? This journey was different from that journey of 1850, when youth, hope and life were before him. Life he knew; it had been lived. More than he hoped had come to him of success, honor, fortune, fame, power, love. And love rode West with him in 1891. Did he recall that other journey of forty-one years ago? Or was it all darkness? Or was it more vivid, more real, and with a purpose at last understood, that while he existed in the flesh he could not understand? Did he again live that long journey? Was he once more a plainsman? Did he cross countless rivers—the Kansas, the Big Blue and the Platte? Was it another hard pull up the Rockies? Did he thirst in hot deserts? With young giant strength did he struggle upward over the snowy Sierra? Did he sense the red soil in the homeland of California? And did he once more find rest at the trail's end in Pleasant Valley?

California was waiting for her adopted son. As the train came down through the Sierra, so often trod by George Hearst, at little way stations groups of silent mourners were gathered in appreciation of a great heart that no longer beat. Men there were, white-haired, like the dead man, who had worked with him and struggled and failed, but tears unashamed streamed down their cheeks; their friend was gone. All through the foothills and in the valley of the Sacramento this happened.

Governor Markham, who had served in Congress with Senator Hearst, had sent the following communication to both houses of the Legislature: "Having been informed of the death of Honorable George Hearst, Senator from this state to the Congress of the United States, I desire to express to you, as a co-ordinate branch of the State Government, my respect for the dead and my sympathy for the bereaved family. He was a well-known pioneer and prominently identified with the early development of the state when hardship and toil were required from everyone, from which he did not shrink. He afterward attained affluence and became prominent in all matters affecting the interests of the public, and by his energy, upright dealing and great business capacity became a prominent factor in the commercial and political history of the state. In each and every phase he was the same kind and thoughtful friend. In his capacity as Senator he was honest, faithful, and intelligent and was highly appreciated by his colleagues in the Senate of the United States."

The Legislature adjourned out of respect. More than half its members went to San Francisco for the funeral.

There was sadness in many hearts, for a kindly, brave, genuine, loyal friend had gone. He had been one of the rulers of America, but had not lost the common touch. He always remained a great democrat, plain George Hearst. San Francisco knew this, and San Francisco royally took back her own. The mighty gathered to say farewell, and the humble also stood by his bier with their last remembrances. Hundreds came, too, from the interior of California, Nevada, Utah, Montana and Arizona. Wherever he had been, George Hearst made friends. They thronged the Grace Episcopal Church, where he lay in state from Thursday, March 12, until Sunday, March 15, guarded day and night by the Third Infantry of the National Guard. The last day it rained, but thousands patiently lingered in the street trying to get a last glimpse of this great Caifornian.

Final services were held in Grace Church, the Reverend R. C. Foute, Rector, officiating. George Hearst's life was summed up in his favorite hymn, sung during the services, "Just As I Am." The honorary pallbearers who went with him to peaceful and beautiful Laurel Hill were Governor H. H. Markham, Mayor George Sanderson, Judge Seldon S. Wright, William D. English, Charles N. Felton, Lloyd Tevis, Jeremiah Lynch, William F. Goad, A. P. Williams, George C. Perkins, Irving M. Scott, Frank McCoppin, Judge Niles Searls, Arthur Rodgers, Louis Sloss, John H. Wise, A. B. Butler, Barry Baldwin, Captain C. L. Taylor, General John Gibbon, Admiral Benham, Russell J. Wilson, Major R. P. Hammond, Jr., E. G. Waite, Irwin G. Stump, Judge J. P. Hoge, Edward McGettigan, Judge R. S. Mesick, J. P. Le Count, A. N. Towne, Judge William T. Wallace, Judge J. V. Coffey, William H. Crocker, Judge R. C. Harrison, Louis Glass, and Judge William H. Beatty.

As soon as the Hearsts acquired a mausoleum at Cypress Lawn in San Mateo County, all that remained of George Hearst was transferred from Laurel Hill to his final home, where he was to await the coming of his wife and beloved companion. Phoebe Hearst had much to do before she was to go, a quarter of a century later, to her husband's side to rest. George Hearst left his widow all his great fortune, requesting her to carry on the good deeds they together had planned.

For twenty-five years Phoebe Hearst was the hostess

of San Francisco and northern California. She gave endlessly to the young and old, to friends, acquaintances, strangers. Millions passed through her hands uncounted. She became the exquisite fairy-godmother of the University of California. Dressed in lavender or gray or purple, she entertained all the students. Her home was their home. She called them by name. She counseled them. She became their friend. She sent them abroad. She developed writers, artists and architects. She paid professors' salaries. She bought equipment for laboratories. She financed archeological expeditions. She erected buildings. Her name finally became a California benediction.

The building that meant most to Phoebe Apperson Hearst was erected as a cenotaph to her husband. It was begun November 18, 1902. Her heart, their united lives, were its cornerstone. Graven on a bronze tablet at the entrance to the Hearst Memorial Mining Building of the University of California are the following words in which Phoebe Hearst summed up her husband's life:

"This building stands as a memorial to George Hearst, a plain, honest man and good miner. The stature and mold of his life bespoke the pioneers who gave their strength to riskful search in the hard places of the earth. He had a warm heart toward his fellow men and his hand was ready to kindly deed. Taking his wealth from the hills, he filched from no man's store and lessened no man's opportunity."

## FROM THE PRESS

The New York *Times* said: "Mr. Hearst was a kind-hearted man, lavish in his expenditures for the relief of the poor, and it is said he never forgot his old friends. Said the correspondent of the *Times* in 1886: 'I have personally seen him on more than one occasion leave a party of broadcloth men to step across the street and shake hands with some ragged wreck of a pioneer whom he had known in early days.' He was a man of good sense, quick perception and excellent judgment, and had clearly defined ideas upon all public questions which he had the faculty of expounding in unmistakable terms. When with his intimates he was a delightful companion, full of good nature and accustomed to deliver himself of many wise, original and homely thoughts and phrases. He was quite free from affectation."

The New York *Tribune* wrote that Mr. Hearst was known as the "patient Senator . . . "

In its column usually devoted to turf matters the New York *World* said: " . . . Senator Hearst rarely bet on his own horses, and, although he was a familiar figure at the clubhouses of the big tracks, he was practically unknown in the ring. He was universally beloved for his kindly gentle ways and his unostentatious manners. 'Uncle George,' as he was lovingly called, had a pleasant way for everybody, and in these days of rampant snobbishness his old-fashioned Democracy was as refreshing as dew in the desert. While the great people are mourning in Washington there is many a wet eye down among the humble stable boys at Sheepshead and Gravesend."

From the San Francisco *Chronicle*: " . . . George Hearst was so prominently identified with the pristine interest of California, mining, that his memory will linger as long as men search for the hidden treasures which the kindly earth conceals. Long before he had turned his attention to politics he was known as one of the very best mining experts on the Pacific Coast, and his very large fortune was acquired in an entirely legitimate way by the exercise of a judgment trained by careful observation and ripened by a large and varied experience.

"Of Senator Hearst's private and domestic relations it is enough to say that he leaves a widow who will honor and revere his memory and a son who gladly acknowledges the infinite debt he owes to an ever kind and indulgent father. The kindest sympathies of all Californians must go out to that widow and son in their affliction, and all differences of opinion, political or otherwise, must be silenced in the presence of death. Under the Act of Congress the Legislature of California now in session must fill the vacancy caused by the death of Senator Hearst upon the second Tuesday after information of the occurring of the vacancy, which, in the natural order of events, will be the 10th of March. A Republican will succeed Senator Hearst, and it is sincerely to be hoped that the choice of the Legislature may fall upon some one who is as thoroughly a Californian and as much devoted to her material interests as was George Hearst."

The San Francisco *Examiner* had the following editorial: " . . . George Hearst had a genius for affairs. A comparatively poor man until middle life, his years had been one sustained determination to meet or make opportunity. When it came he seized it with a mastering hand and quickly became a financial power. There was in him the rare capacity to conceive and organize great enterprises and to conduct many at once. Though of a highly strung temperament, no one ever saw him excited about a matter of business. The greater the stake and the more critical the emergency, the calmer and clearer of brain he became. At a danger point his were the nerve, the phlegm and the daring decision of mind of a great general when the battle wavers . . .

"But it is not as the penetrating mining expert, the organizer of gigantic enterprises, or the possessor of immense wealth that he will be mourned. It is the simple truth, and not an obituary commonplace, that his death will carry pain to the multitude of hearts . . . While he had a singularly keen perception of character and a shrewdness that baffled all pretenders, his heart was tender and his charity great. His capacity for forgiveness was inexhaustible. Neither in business, politics nor private life would he cherish enmities — though when blows were going he would give as well as take, for he was a man of an intense and masculine nature. But the conflict over, he was for shaking hands, with a good humor that had in it no admixture of guile. If he has left enemies he passed away hating none . . .

"A strong man, an able man, a good and very human man, has been taken away in George Hearst. He had a manly, a gentle and a loving heart. There will be moist eyes in unnumbered Western homes, grand and humble, at the news of his death; and the sorrow will not be least in the cabins dotting the canyons and streams of the Sierras."

The sentiments of the whole people of the West were happily expressed in the following lines from the pen of Mr. Frank H. Gassaway, one of California's brightest and most famous poets, published a few days after the death of Senator Hearst:

"Earth's great ones may sorrow beside him
 And over his catafalque bend,
But we — we who knew him and tried him —
 The statesman mourn not, but the friend.

For our comrade he was from the hour
 He toiled in the ranks by our side;
The hand that grasped riches and power
 Forgot not the pick that it plied.

And surely, if deeds of sweet pity
 Are treasured for recompense meet,
The path to the beautiful city
 Is smooth to his home-faring feet.

Then let his chief mourners, the lowly,
 With tears he so often repressed,
The face of our dead cover slowly,
 And bear him away to his rest.

And though 'tis an omen that ever
 Shall soften the pang of regret —
The great heart shall beat again, never,
 The smile on his face lingers yet.

Lingers yet — and we know 'tis a token,
 From the shores where the purified dwell,
The Master's 'well done' has been spoken,
 We may bid him 'good night,' for all's well."

# INDEX

Hearst, George *(Cont.)*
48; journey overland, 49-59; sick with cholera, 60; continues journey westward, 61-66; arrives at Fort Bridger, 67-68; takes Humbolt River route, 69-71, 73-75; reaches California, 76-79; hunts for mining opportunities, 81-82; mines at Jackass Gulch, 83-84; goes to Grass Valley, 85-86; business man at Nevada City, 87-88; finds Merrimac ledge, 90-91; goes into business at Sacramento, 93; returns to Nevada City, 94-95; goes to Washoe mining area, 96, 99; buys interest in Ophir, at Gold Hill, 103-104; takes Comstock ore to San Francisco, 105-106; returns to Missouri, 110-114; marries Phoebe Elizabeth Apperson, 115; returns to California, 117-123; goes back to Comstock, 124-125; litigation over Ophir claims, 126-128; buys house on Chestnut Street, San Francisco, 129; elected to Legislature, 131-136; abandons Comstock, 137; deals in San Francisco real estate, 138; goes back to mining and mine appraisals, 139-140; invests in Nevada properties, 141-144; goes to Utah, 145-147; buys Ontario Mine, 148-151, 153; buys Homestake Mine, 154-158; description of, 159-161; his mining interests, 162; buys into Anaconda, 163-167; land acquisitions, 169; buys Piedra Blanca Ranch, 170-171; other purchases, 172-176; purchases *San Francisco Examiner,* 177-183; deeds newspaper to son, William Randolph Hearst, 184-185; nominated for governor of California, 187-190; loses to George Stoneman, 191-194; appointed to U.S. Senate, 195-203; experiences with President Grover Cleveland, 205-208; returned to U.S. Senate, 209-213; congressional efforts in behalf of California, 215-223, 225; illness, 226; his death,

Hearst, George *(Cont.)*
227; funeral, 228-230; memorial, 231; press eulogy, 232-235
Hearst, John, 15
Hearst, John III, 14
Hearst, Joseph, 15
Hearst, Margaret, 15
Hearst, Martha ("Patsy"), 23, 33-34, 40, 46-48, 58, 83, 109, 112
Hearst, Mary, 15
Hearst, Mary O'Brien, 15
Hearst, Millicent Willson, 9
Hearst, Philip, 23-24, 30, 32-34, 38
Hearst, Phoebe Apperson, 11, 34, 46, 113-115, 117-124, 128, 133, 136, 139, 149-151, 155, 158, 160, 166-167, 172, 193, 196-197, 210-213, 227, 230, 231
Hearst, Robert, 15
Hearst, Thomas, 15
Hearst, William, 15
Hearst, William G., 15, 17-22, 24, 27, 30, 32-33
Hearst, William Randolph, 9-12, 124, 149, 159, 170, 172, 179-181, 183-185, 226, 227
Hemstead, C. H., 107
Henderson, A. B., 183
Hermes Mine, 142-143
Homestake Mine, 155-159, 161
Homestake Mining Company, 156-158
Humboldt River, 68, 73-74
Humboldt Sink, 74
Hurst, Alicia, 14
Hurst, James, 14
Hurst, John, 14
Hust, John Jr., 14
Hurst, Mary, 14
Hurst, Philip, 14 ·
Hurst, Walter, 14
Hurst, William, 14

Independence, Missouri, 49
Independence Rock, 65

Jackass Gulch, 10, 82-84, 87
Johnston, George Pendleton, 178-179